The Art of Being Invisible

by

JYOTHSNA KASU

The Art of Being Invisible

Identify Cyber Threats in Real-Time
Protect Yourself & Your Family.

JYOTHSNA KASU

To my loving husband, Prabhakar Kasu,

& my adorable son Aryan Kasu

CONTENTS

Section – I

Section - II

About the Author

Jyothsna Kasu has spent a career in Human Resources and Technology. She has over 15 years of experience working in a large, matrix-structured, global team environment with a wide range of technologies. She consistently took on challenges across start-ups and large businesses, helping them build organizational processes and cultures that enable growth and excellence.

Her enriched experience working with diverse teams across Manufacturing, Electronics, Consulting & IT/ITES industry verticals has made her a significant contributor to building and grooming talent during the rapid growth phase at multiple organizations during her early years. Her urge to learn never stopped her from getting to the bottom of what technology is all about. She believes that learning never stops and life always has something to teach us, thus making learning and sharing her passion.

Preface

Suddenly, there have been massive data hacks, privacy breaches, unauthorised disclosure of data and inappropriate sharing of personal and sensitive information, where the whole world is waking up to the importance of data privacy. The phase of the Information life-cycle is changing rapidly, when a company collects our personal data it is liable to protect their consumers/ customers sensitive data, but the recent study says that there is a new victim of identity theft every 2 seconds in the United States alone. Privacy is now a must in today's digital data-sharing and technological economy. Rise of smart devices, Internet of Things (IoT), Artificial Intelligence (AI), accelerated pace of mobile app usage and social media sites have pushed the boundaries of privacy- invasiveness and data breaches continue to proliferate giving rise to cybercrimes. As society and technology is evolving so are we co - evolving. Explosion of technology has put us through new challenges and the impact of digital surge has made it inevitable for us to use digital technologies during this Covid-19 pandemic. As digitization disrupts society ever more profoundly, with Internet governance, digital money etc., concern is growing too. Concerns about jobs, wages, inequality, health, resource efficiency and finally security. This book addresses digital security concerning every person, and my journey and passion to learn has given me a chance to understand cybersecurity and I believe in sharing my knowledge. So this is an effort to share and create awareness, for those who are keen on knowing, learning and being vigilant. While Big data is following us and capturing every move of ours, we need to be prudent. This book has two sections, the first section talks about few technical jargons in the world of cybersecurity, the second section is about the fast evolving technological changes, Social engineering, Future Crimes, Deep Web, Deepfakes and Cyber Privacy. Hoping that this book could throw light creating awareness, addressing privacy concerns and giving readers the knowledge of few privacy laws that are available today.

Chapter 1
Evolution of Technology

The word Secure is derived from the Latin word "secures," meaning freedom from anxiety. Se means "without," and cure means "care." Ancient security system highlights the physical safety of people, their loved ones and their hard-earned possessions. The first residential security system network was created in 1874, but ancient security systems existed long before. Few of those outdated security systems are still in use today. Some old security systems like Moats, Walls, Gates, Watchtowers, and Weapons are used in remote, underdeveloped villages till today. Each generation of residents becomes safer as home security systems incorporate new technology. Some things never changed, and the need for physical and home security still exists. From the dawn of civilization to the present day, every homeowner has been fighting for the safety of loved ones and their hard-earned possessions, guarding against intruders who would harm and steal from them.

Let's jump into technology and see how it evolved. The electronic calculator has been a portable electronic device used to perform calculations. The first pocket-sized calculator was created in the 1960s to perform calculations ranging from basic arithmetic to complex mathematics with some limitations. Most calculators cannot handle numbers more significant than $9.99999999 \times 10^{99}$. Numbers beyond the value create an overflow error. Computers were invented to carry on much more complex calculations with higher memory and storage capacity to encounter this problem. Computers now have inbuilt calculators and can store up to or more than one terabyte, 1000 gigabytes.

Each era's technology evolved and changed to different shapes and sizes; all four Industrial revolutions varied and helped people use technology to make their lives easier and better by perfecting it and bringing it to the next level. The first Industrial revolution in 1765 saw the helped agricultural societies become more industrialized and urban, the invention of the steam engine due to massive extraction of coal. Steam engines accelerated the economy by assisting people in speeding up the process of manufacturing transcontinental railroads. Other inventions like the cotton gin, electricity accelerated growth and permanently changed society. A century later, the world went through a second Industrial revolution in 1870 with massive technological advancement and transformation with new energy sources like electricity, gas, and oil. The Second Industrial revolution saw growth in the machine tool industry, manufacturing interchangeable parts, and the invention of the Bessemer process to produce steel. Improvement and development in manufacturing and production technology enabled widespread technological systems like telegraph, gas, water supply, railroad network, water supply, and sewage system. Telephones and electrical power were the most effective technical systems that were introduced during this revolution. The 17th and 18th centuries saw the first steam-powered self-propelled vehicles. The invention of the automobile and the plane at the beginning of the 20th century is considered the most important achievement and created a landmark in history, making the second industrial revolution a significant one. In the second half of the 20th century, the emergence of Nuclear energy, electronics, telecommunication, and computers made ways to space expeditions, research, and biotechnology. The shift from mechanical, analog electronics technology to digital electronics is called the digital revolution.

The third industrial revolution saw automation and digitization through electronics, computers, the Internet, and nuclear energy. Due to this shift to digitization, the third industrial revolution is also known as the digital revolution. Two significant inventions, Programmable Logic Controller (PLCs) and Robots during the third industrial revolution, helped rise to an era of high-level automation. Programmable Logic Controller (PLCs) is an industrial digital computer that controls the manufacturing processes. The robot is capable of automatically carrying out a complex series of actions by mimicking a lifelike appearance. The Fourth Industrial Revolution is building on the Third, the digital revolution, and evolving exponentially. The fourth industrial revolution, also known as Industry 4.0, is driven by big data analytics, the Internet of things (IoT), high-speed mobile Internet, Artificial Intelligence (AI), cloud technology, 3D printing, quantum computing, genetic engineering, and many other technologies. The technologies used in the fourth industrial revolution are changing our personal and professional lives drastically. The global labor market is increasingly adopting new technology, making it easier for companies to automate routine tasks disrupting the balance between humans' job responsibilities versus machines and algorithms. Transformations and disruptions in the labor market due to innovative technologies worldwide could significantly impact our society and workforce. Industry 4.0 involves adopting cyber-physical systems like the Internet of things (IoT) and the Internet of systems. A Cyber-physical system (CPS) is a computer system that integrates sensing, computing, control, and networking into physical objects and infrastructure, connecting them through the Internet. CPS is an engineering discipline that is focused on technology, having a solid foundation in mathematical abstraction. Some examples of CPS are medical monitoring, Industrial Internet, Smart grids, smart cities, Smart banking, Smart cars, smart homes, "Smart" Anything that's physically interconnected through the Internet. The IoT environment still has many security challenges to overcome; some of the obstacles are manufacturing standards, software attacks, user knowledge, awareness, physical device hardening, and IoT device management.

Manufacturing standards: The IoT market is growing every year and is expected to grow significantly. In 2018 there were 7 billion IoT devices; the number of IoT devices reached 26.66 billion in 2019. Every second, 127 new IoT devices are connected to the Web, according to McKinsey's report. A report from IoT business news confirms 21.7 billion active connected devices worldwide, and their forecast for 2025 is 31 billion connected IoT devices. With the growing IoT market, compliance with IoT manufacturers plays a vital role in addressing security issues. Every manufacturer needs to spend enough time and resources on security and undiscovered vulnerabilities. These vulnerabilities can expose information of the IoT consumers, and every hack would enable hackers to gain entry to spread Malware. A smart refrigerator can disclose personal information like a consumer's Google login credentials, and an intelligent vacuum flaw could give hackers access to cameras and know your in-house locations. A recent example where the security researchers revealed vulnerabilities in Trifo Iron pie smart vacuum cleaner having a built-in camera could let hackers access the video stream remotely. By exploiting vulnerabilities, hackers could potentially take control of a smart vacuum cleaner. A smart lightbulb system could be hacked to gain access to your network, Amazon's Ring security could share your data with Facebook and Google. A smart Biometric padlock can be hacked in seconds and accessed with a Bluetooth key with the same MAC address as the padlock device. An inexperienced hacker with little expertise can hack and access buildings' smart-control. They can also launch distributed denial-of-service (DDoS) attacks, disrupting the service and making it inoperable. Attackers actively try to exploit the door access controller system. Nortek Security & Control (NSC) was targeted, leaving more than 2300 buildings affected by the hack, putting properties and companies behind the structures at risk.

In December 2019, the Ring security camera was hacked. The hacker accessed the Ring camera inside an 8-year-old girl›s bedroom in Mississippi and claimed to be Santa Claus, spying on the house and terrifying the girl. «Evil Corp,» a Russian hacking group that stole $ 100 million from banks using malicious software that swiped banking credentials, Russian cybercriminal Aleksandr Brovko and an active member involved in hacking, was sentenced to eight years by a US District judge. In another case, on September 7, 2020, BancoEstado, one of Chile›s three biggest banks, was forced to shut down all the bank branches due to a ransomware attack.

Software attacks: IoT software attacks can exploit the entire system interconnected, steal information, alter data, compromise and damage devices and deny services.

Generic Cybercrimes:

Software piracy, stealing passwords and usernames, Network intrusions, Social engineering, Posting or Transmitting illegal material, Dumpster diving, Malicious code, unauthorized destruction of information, Embezzlement, Data-Diddling, etc.

2021 Internet usage statistics show that approximately 4.93 billion people out of the current worldwide estimated population of 7.8 billion have access to the Internet frequently, which means 63.2% of the world population uses the Internet. Asia accounts for most internet users, with 2.6 billion people making it 51.8% of the global internet population. Europe accounts for 14.8%, and North America accounts for 7.2%. North America and Europe are the two regions globally with the highest penetration rates; 90.3% of North America and 87.2% of Europe have access to the Internet daily. With 127 million websites available, 306 billion emails being sent per day, and social network users in millions using platforms like Facebook, YouTube, Instagram, etc.., global internet traffic reaches 235.7 Exabytes per month in 2021. With this kind of Internet usage outburst, Cybercrimes like Identity Theft, Software attacks, Generic crimes will also rise.

Can we avoid these attacks and unauthorized access? Yes, we can with the help of cybersecurity. Cybersecurity is the art of protecting networks, network devices, and data from unauthorized access. It is also a practice of ensuring confidentiality, integrity, and availability of information. Due to digitization, most communication and transactions rely on digital smart devices like smartphones, tablets, laptops, computers, and internet connectivity. Given the pandemic, a significant part of our daily life depends on technology, and people are dependent on technology, and it›s become an integral part of everyone›s lives. Technology is in everything we do today - communication, banking, shopping, entertainment, and health. Over the years, technology has continued to improve in society; as technology continues to improve, society becomes more dependent on artificial intelligence (AI). Our personal information is stored either in our smartphones, tablet, computer, or on someone else›s system. Data about family members' names, salary, and shopping habits could be available online depending on information anyone has revealed during the surveys or social engineering sites, or eCommerce sites.

The Internet knows a person's age, address, profession, income, and marital status. This information available online creates a digital identity. Online search activity, electronic transactions, username, password, medical history, purchase history, date of birth, and social security number populate digital identities, making it impossible to control. Most countries lack data-privacy legislation. People are not protected against rampant data brokering on the world's leading data gathering and analytics sites like Verisk, Axion LLC, Oracle Data Cloud, Epsilon Data Management LLC, and Experian PLC. Some background check sites like Been Verified, People Looker, Truth finder, White pages, etc., could publish your information online, and anyone can buy it for a price. Past and present data of people are collected, stored, preserved, and sold for a fee. With plans starting less than $30/month, companies offer various affordable options and allow you to choose the kind of subscription you want to access personal profiles, information, and professional emails.

Once the information is obtained from the public domain, cybercriminals can deploy various attacks against individual victims or businesses to access the data making people or businesses the victims of identity theft. Besides making smart cyber defense choices, solid cyber defense technology can protect people from security vulnerabilities and be identity theft victims.

Let us understand how one could be a victim; Number of Digital buyers is increasing, and 2021 statistics show that mobile eCommerce sales account for approximately 72.9% of all online purchases, totaling 3.56 trillion dollars.

Let's take a simple example of an online shopping site, say **www.Amazon.com** or **www. eBay.com**. Most of us store our personal and financial information to make our shopping experience easy and faster. We keep our address, email-id, and banking details on the shopping app or website. This information is stored on the server, and any cybercriminal could access this information. Sometimes we receive emails or gift vouchers for shopping, and that's where we need to watch out. To obtain the coupon code, we may be asked to fill in our credentials; here, there are two possibilities. It could be genuine for verification. Secondly, it could be an act of cyber-attack to get your credentials. If it's a fake email, the hacker is trying to get your credentials for unauthorized access to misuse or wipe off your bank account balance. We can be vigilant, avoid such attacks, and always watch out before filling in your credentials online. Let us try and understand different categories of cyber-attacks:

Operating system (OS) attack: Attackers find the Operating system (OS) vulnerabilities and exploit them. OS vulnerabilities could include errors made by the installer while installing OS by not focusing on defaults and leaving the ports open. Administrators account with no passwords. Some of the examples are buffer overflow, unpatched systems.

Misconfiguration attacks: Attack targeted towards the database, networks, web servers, application platforms that are on purpose or accidentally not configured appropriately for security. The admin's system leaves security settings at the lowest possible level, enables every service, and opens all firewall ports that could be the target. It happens due to the misconfiguration of the deployed devices or system.

Shrink Wrap Code Attacks: Using default, built-in code and scripts off-the-shelf applications, these scripts and code off-the-shelf are designed to make installation and administration easier lead to vulnerabilities if not managed.

Application-level attacks: Attacks targeted towards the actual programming code and software logic of an application. Many applications on the network are not tested for vulnerabilities built into them. e.g., SQL injection. Buffer overflow, cross-site scripting, path traversal, local file inclusion, parameter tampering, distributed Denial of Service.

SQL Injection is a code injection technique where you view, edit, and delete tables from databases. SQL injection attacks allow attackers to spoof identity, tamper with existing data, cause repudiation issues such as voiding transactions or changing balances, destroy the data, make it unavailable and become the administrators of the database server. Some joint SQL injections are retrieving confidential data, modifying SQL query, changing the query to interfere with the application logic, and retrieving data from different database tables.

Cross-site scripting (XSS) is a web security vulnerability that allows an attacker to compromise users' interactions with vulnerable applications. Malicious code or scripts are injected into websites and web applications to control and run the end users' devices. Attackers could send the victim a misleading email with a link containing malicious JavaScript. If the victim clicks on the link, the HTTP request is initiated from the victim's browser and sent to the vulnerable web application. Typical XSS attacks include session stealing, account takeover, attacks on the user's browser such as malicious software downloads, keylogging, Multi-Factor Authentication, and Web Application Firewall bypass, and client-side attack.

Path Traversal (or directory traversal is also known as. / (dot dot slash)) attack is a web security vulnerability that allows an attacker to access and read files on the server running an application. An HTTP exploit allows an attacker to access restricted files, directories, and commands that reside outside of the web server›s root directory. An attacker might manipulate a URL so that the website will reveal the confined files on the webserver.

The local File Inclusion (LFI) attack is a file inclusion vulnerability; LFI allows an attacker to include files on a server through the web browser. LFI is an inclusion attack through which an attacker can trick the web application into having files on the target web server by exploiting functionality that dynamically includes local files or scripts. LFI attack uses local files on the target server when carrying the attack and can affect companies and organizations with poorly written web applications or websites. With Remote file inclusion (RFI), the attacker uses a remote file on the target server instead of a local file to execute the malicious script. With the correct privileges, the attacker will pull all the sensitive information from the target website or server.

Distributed denial-of-service attack or DDoS attack is a malicious attempt to disrupt a targeted server's regular traffic. It occurs when multiple systems are flooded with a targeted system's bandwidth or resources, usually one or more web servers. DDoS uses more than one unique IP address or machine, often from thousands of hosts infected with Malware.

Parameter tampering is a web-based attack where certain parameters in the URL (Uniform Resource Locator) or web page form field data entered by a user is changed without the user's authorization. Parameter tampering attack manipulates parameters exchanged between the Client and server to modify application data, such as user credentials, permissions, price, or other information. For example, an online shopping site uses hidden fields to refer to its products/items:

Here the value 150.00 can be changed or modified by the hacker, lowering the cost, which is a loss to the eCommerce site.

Chapter 2
Malware attack

The term malware is short for malicious software, which is designed to perform evil and disruptive actions. It executes unauthorized activities on the victim's system. The intention is to capture information about the victim; Malware programs install a keylogger on a network. Keyloggers are monitoring software designed to record the keystrokes made by the user. They capture the keystrokes as they enter. Some of the most common ways computers get infected with spyware include accepting a prompt or pop-up without reading it, downloading software from an unreliable source, pirating media such as movies, music, or games, opening email attachments from unknown senders.

Worms are standalone malicious code or programs that can self-replicate and propagate independently as soon as they have breached the system. Unlike the virus's worms do not necessarily require any user interaction to function; they replicate extremely rapidly across networks and hosts and consume a lot of memory.

The virus is a specific type of malware that self-replicates by inserting its code into other programs. A virus requires some user action to initiate its infectious activity. The virus can be activated when a victim opens the infected application or file. Some of the deadliest computer viruses and worms are ILOVEYOU, Crptolocker, Melissa, My doom, Stuxnet, WannaCry, SQL Slammer, Storm Worm, Code Red, etc.

Bot (abbreviation for "robot") is an automated program or application programmed to do specific tasks and designed to run over the Internet. Bots do repetitive tasks and are automatic; they often imitate or replace a human user's behavior and run according to their instructions without a human user's initiation. There are two types of bots, good bots and bad bots. Search engine bots that crawl the worldwide Web to find updated content that improves search engine results are promising. Chatbots which perform an automated task like setting the alarm, telling weather report or searching online is help bots, Siri and Cortana are help bots. Googlebot, the Baidu spider, bingbot, and yandexbot are some of the well-known good bots. Bad bots are bots that perform malicious acts, steal data or damage networks or sites with malware.

Ransomware is typically spread through phishing emails that contain malicious attachments or when a user unknowingly visits an infected website. Ransomware is malicious software designed to deny or restrict access to computer systems, files, folders, or data until a ransom is paid to restore the access. Habana Labs, an Intel-owned AI processor developer that accelerates artificial intelligence workloads in the data center, suffered a cyberattack where data was stolen and leaked by threat actors. Ransom payment requested was typically between 7 and 9 Bitcoins, which translated to somewhere between $135K and $173K.

A rootkit is a form of malware designed to stay undetected on the computer. Cybercriminals use a rootkit to gain control over target devices or computer systems and remotely access them. Rootkit installation can be automated; hackers can install rootkit after obtaining administrator access and modify existing software. Most rootkits affect the software and the operating system, but some can also infect hardware and firmware. Rootkit detection is challenging and even more challenging to remove.

Spyware is malware installed on a computing device without the end user's knowledge and has been designed to gather information about the system in a stealthy manner. Spyware tracks websites you visit, files you download, location, emails, contact details, personal and payment information, user id, and passwords. They also capture keyboard outputs and report activity, and provide information to a third party without your consent. Some of the Spywares are adware, system monitors, web tracking, and trojans.

Adware (advertising-supported software) is a type of malware that delivers advertisements, mostly pop-up ads on websites. Advertisements show up in places they shouldn't be, web browsers homepage changes without permission. The most common adware ways to infect the PCs are browser extensions, toolbars, bundled software, and free downloads offered by pop-ups. System Monitor is a type of spyware that can capture everything you do on the computer system monitors. They can record all keystrokes, emails, chat-room dialogs, and websites visited, programs run, contacts saved, login, passwords, and system monitors have been disguised as freeware.

Web tracking is a type of spyware that monitors and tracks Web, cookies, websites, internet usage, credit card and bank information, personal identity, private browsing activity, browsing history, and every user's activity on the Web.

Trojan spyware is often installed unknowingly due to installing some other software or is delivered by an exploit to harm the user's system. The trojan is a software application that has been designed to provide covert access to the victim's system. These programs or applications are similar to Troy's ancient story where the Trojan horse led to Troy's fall. The Greeks presented the Trojans with a giant hollow wooden Trojan horse as a peace offering to Troy. But the Trojan horse had elite Greek soldiers hidden inside; while Troy's city slept, Greek soldiers emerged from the horse and attacked Troy. The trojan is a malicious code packaged to appear harmless, but its goals are similar to the virus or worm to control the system and perform malicious tasks.

Mobile Malware is Malware that infects mobiles and smartphones. Mobile Malware works the same as any other malware. Some of the applications, wireless technologies, and processes that could affect mobile devices are Apps, Bluetooth, and jailbreaking, respectively. We frequently download new apps to our mobile phones. Apps ask for geolocation, camera, and microphone access while downloading, and once the permission has been granted, malicious code can be injected into the smartphone. Any app carrying malicious code can now easily spy on us, silently collecting information. Any older version of the operating system on the mobile can infect the mobile phone through Bluetooth. Jailbreak means allowing the phone to gain full access to the operating system's root and access all features by removing the limitations. Jailbreaking has also been called rooting due to removing the mobile or tablet constraints running the Android operating system. When you jailbreak Apple devices, you lose the Apple manufacturer's security protections, opening the security holes that may undermine the device's built-in security measures.

Polymorphic Malware is a difficult-to-locate infection and one of the sophisticated classes of malware. It constantly changes its identifiable features to evade detection. Every time polymorphic malware infects a file, it adjusts parts of itself to make it difficult to detect. Using advanced security techniques and the Pattern analysis method is the most dependable way to identify and detect this malware.

Scareware is a scam and a new type of malware. Cybercriminals attempt to access computers by scaring and warning the victim of potential harm that could befall them if they don't take some action immediately. Scareware is a malware tactic that tricks users into believing that they need to download or buy software to protect their computers. Scareware uses social engineering sites to take advantage of a user's fear, coaxing them into installing fake antivirus software. They aim to gain access to the victim's credit card information by tricking the victim into buying antivirus software.

Social Engineering is a non-technical strategy hackers use to break into standard security practices. Social engineering relies heavily on human interaction and involves tactics to trick and create trust in people to gain legitimate, authorized access to confidential information. Social engineering can be through email or misdirection of web pages. It can be done in person by an insider or an outside entity or over the phone. Some social engineering techniques are phishing attack, spear-phishing attack, whale phishing attack, pretexting, pharming, mal advertising, SMS phishing, Voice phishing, shoulder surfing, USB key drop, Elicitation, interrogation, and Impersonation.

Phishing is a fraudulent practice of sending emails to obtain personal or sensitive information, such as social security numbers, usernames, passwords, financial details, and other sensitive data, by impersonating oneself as a legitimate entity through digital communication. Phishing campaigns don't target victims individually, and they are sent in bulk. Phishing scams can lead to personal and sensitive information getting published on the dark Web, and the information could fall into the wrong hands. People can be victims of Identity theft and financial fraud. Personal information is often sold on the dark web, and the researchers have listed the average price tags attached to stolen personal data, which can be found on the Dark web price index, for example, American express cards with PIN could cost US$35, credit card details sell for US$ 12-20. Dark web monitoring services could be one way to protect yourself from being a victim.

Spear phishing is highly targeted and targets specific individuals, organizations, businesses, or companies in contrast to bulk phishing. Whaling is a spear-phishing attack aimed at high-profile senior executives such as CFO or CEO masquerading as a legitimate email. Most whaling instances manipulate the victim into permitting high-worth wire transfer to the attackers. Vishing is a phishing form; it's a phone scam with a combination of voice and phishing. The goal here is similar to phishing to steal someone's identity, information or money.

A drive-by attack is a malicious program that installs on your devices without your consent. It's a standard method of spreading malware. Hackers look for insecure websites and plant malicious scripts into HTTP or PHP code on one of the pages. This code may install malware directly onto the victim's computer or re-direct the victim to a site controlled by the cybercriminal. The script or the code has been often obfuscated to make it difficult for security researchers to analyze the code; such attacks infect the computers automatically and silently if the computer is vulnerable in some way.

A password attack is an attempt to decrypt or obtain a user's password with malicious intention. There are many ways of cracking a password. Eavesdropping or sniffing is a network security attack where a cybercriminal tries to steal the information transmitted over network-connected digital devices like computers, smartphones, etc. The episode is made in two ways: active eavesdropping. The attacker makes independent connections with the victim like MITM, where hackers disguise and listen to digital or analog voice communications directly, secondly passive eavesdropping where attackers need not have to be on any ongoing connection with the victim. A software piece can simply be sitting in the network path and capturing all relevant network traffic for later analysis.

A Brute-Force attack is a cryptographic hack that relies on guessing possible combinations of a targeted password until the correct password is discovered. This attack needs an exhaustive search. If the password longer, more prolonged, the password more varieties will have to be tested by the attacker or hacker. The best way to block brute-force attacks is to lock out accounts after defined numbers of incorrect password attempts, and it's better to keep them locked until manually unlocked by an administrator.

A Birthday attack is a statistical phenomenon that makes brute forcing on one-way hashes easy. A brute force attack is a trial-and-error method to guess login information or encryption keys. Still, a birthday attack is a type of cryptographic attack that exploits the mathematics behind the birthday problem in probability theory. Attackers can use this to abuse communication between two or more parties. In a room of 23 people, the probability of sharing the birthday with any other person is greater than 50%. You can continue this logic for n people sharing a birthday with any other of the n people, and you will reach 99.9% probability at about n = 70 people. To get a chance of 99.9%, you need 70 people in the room, and to get 100% probability, you need 366 people. It's best advised to use a powerful combination and a long sequence of bit length to prevent brute-force attacks or Birthday attacks.

Dictionary Network attack is a form of brute-force attack. A dictionary attack uses words from the dictionary to crack the password. It's a program where systematic terms from a list are entered to gain access to a system, account, or encrypted file. It's an attempted illegal entry to a computer system that uses a dictionary headword list to generate possible passwords. With the Internet being rampantly used, millions of password lists are recovered from past data breaches on the open Internet. Cracking software's tools can use lists and produce common variations to gain illegal access into the system. Some of them popular in 2021 are Crack Station, Password Cracker, Brutus, Air crack, John the Ripper, etc.

Keylogger attack is created and then initiated by spyware which captures anything that happens on the keyboard. Keylogging or keystroke logging or keyboard capturing are all the same. It's an act of recording the keys struck on the keyboard covertly so that the targeted victim using the keyboard is unaware that their actions are being monitored. Every word typed by the targeted victim on the keyboard is recorded, and sensitive data can be retrieved by the hacker operating the keylogging program. Keyloggers could be legitimate software or hardware sold in the open market when used for company security by companies for employee time tracking and monitoring. At the same time, parents monitor the kids and law enforcement. They are still a significant threat as they are used for cyber fraud by cybercriminals. Keyloggers get installed by Phishing emails, Trojan viruses, web page scripts, USB, keylogger hardware. It's important to recognize warning signs like computer performance when browsing or starting programs, abnormal delay in activities, pop-ups, new icons on the computer, or any other strange behavior. Being alert and cautious is the best way to protect yourself against keylogger malware. Some of the best keyloggers and monitoring software are Spytech Spy agent, All in One Keylogger, Aramex, PC Pandora, etc.

A Rainbow table attack is a type of hacking where the perpetrator uses a rainbow hash table to crack the passwords stored in a database system. The reason it's called Rainbow Tables is that each column uses a different reduction function. The passwords in a computer system are not stored as plain texts but are hashed using encryption. A hash function is used to generate the new value according to a mathematical algorithm; it maps arbitrary size data to fixed-size values. Hashing is the process of converting a given key into another deal. Hackers prefer rainbow table attacks to Brute-force or dictionary attacks because the former allows them to crack passwords faster. Attackers can use the rainbow attack repeatedly to attack passwords, and the amount of memory needed on the attacking machine is significantly reduced.

Man-the-middle (MITM) attack is when an attacker inserts himself in the middle of the two legitimate participants and interrupts or manipulates an existing conversation or data transfer to retrieve confidential information. The two honest participants may be unaware of the attacker while the attacker acts legitimate and could cause damage by sending malicious links.

AI-Powered attacks are attacks using Artificial Intelligence (AI), and these could be auto-generated attacks. AI has the potential to automate intrusion techniques by launching attacks at unprecedented speed. Additionally, along with AI, Machine Learning (ML) and evolutionary computation algorithms are used. AI-powered Malware could move more quickly through an organization by using ML and evolutionary computation algorithms to probe internal systems without giving itself away. ML has been designed to allow machines to learn from data as opposed to programming. ML is a computer algorithm that improves automatically through experience, and its practical use is to predict outcomes after learning from the data. Although ML has always been considered a form of AI, Machine learning indicates and Artificial Learning acts.

On the other hand, evolutionary computation is used to take all the general information available, analyze it, solve the problems, predict a suitable solution taking action to avoid getting caught during or after the AI attack. These programs could be smart enough to figure out every employee who works or has worked for a company by trawling through LinkedIn data or social network sites. It could then target victims, attack their home network, and wait for them to connect to the corporate network. No firewalls, VPNs, or authentication can stop them from spreading their wings to find the target data. Disrupt, steal or destroy, and it could feasibly succeed in its objective.

The zero-day exploit attack exploits a software or hardware security weakness that the vendor or developer may be unaware of. The term "Zero-Day" refers to the number of days the software vendor knows about the attack. Here the attacker exploits the software and releases malware before the developer has an opportunity to create a patch to fix the vulnerability, and that's why it's called "Zero-Day."

In a Zero-day event, there are 3 phases: Zero-day Vulnerability: It is a software security flaw or flaw in the way software interacts with other software that is unknown or yet to be discovered and patched by the software vendor. Zero-day exploit - An exploit that attacks zero-day vulnerability is called a zero-day exploit, usually malicious software used by cybercriminals to exploit zero-day vulnerability to gain access to a target system and cash in on their schemes. A zero-day attack - is the act of applying a zero-day exploit for personal gains and malicious purposes.

An Insider threat is a malicious threat to the Organization that comes from their employees or people within the Organization like business partners, contractors, or anyone associated with the Organization. An Insider may use their authorized access to gain sensitive information or data to harm the Organization's security.

Today there are more devices connected, and our daily lives depend primarily on technology and connectivity; it's led every individual and Organization alike to rethink how safe their networks are? Now words like threats, vulnerabilities, and exploit have become part of lives too. How do we protect ourselves and our loved ones is the question that everyone needs to find an answer to? The first thing is to be always alert and watch out, Do-not reuse passwords, Do-not believe anyone online and share data or information unless you know them personally, Use two-factor authentication, Use platforms that use end-to-end encryption for data, Don't give up your data on every social networking platform or site, Manage your social media settings, Strengthen your home network, Know what to do if you become a victim, Use personal monitoring service to keep yourself informed when data has been hacked these are few things that could potentially help us stay ahead of complicated problems.

Chapter 3
Introduction to Hacking and Ethical Hacking

Hacking means compromising computer systems, personal accounts, computer networks, or any digital device. Hacking also refers to exploiting system vulnerabilities and compromising security controls to gain unauthorized access to the system. It involves modifying systems or stealing sensitive information from the system. Ethical hacking is an authorized attempt to gain unauthorized access to a computer system, application, or data. Hacker is a person who uses computers and technical knowledge to gain unauthorized access to data. Hackers are intelligent and skilled individuals with excellent computer skills who break into systems and networks to steal data or perform malicious attacks. There are different categories of hackers, and their motives differ; some do for fun and others to commit a crime. Ethical hackers have a code of ethics and make sure that they will cause no harm to the clients and also make sure that the system or network is evaluated correctly for security issues and vulnerabilities. Let's understand different types of hackers and their roles briefly:

Script kiddies are hackers who have limited hacking knowledge or no training; they use existing computer scripts or code to hack into computers, lacking the expertise to write their code. Script Kiddies use basic techniques and tools.

White hat hackers are good guys who protect and keep the data safe from other hackers. They have a code of ethics and use defensive purposes; This group is also called ethical hackers, pen-testers, or security analysts. Their work is legal as they work with the system owner's consent.

Black hat hackers are hackers with malicious intentions. They often steal, exploit and sell data for personal gains. They operate on the opposite side of the law, and black-hat-hacking is a criminal activity.

Gray hat hackers cannot be trusted as they cross into both offensive and defensive actions. They may do both, like fixing vulnerability and exploiting vulnerabilities for fun or to troll. Hacktivists are hackers who promote political agendas by hacking, and they target government agencies and large corporations.

Suicide hackers will perform any attack for a cause and try to knock out a target to prove a point. There would always be individuals who would find ways and certainly aim to bring down the critical infrastructure for a cause. However, these people are not too concerned about facing the consequences of the same.

Cyber terrorists are hackers who are influenced or motivated by certain religious or political beliefs. They work to cause fear and disruption of systems and networks.

Governments recruit State-sponsored hackers to gain access to other governments' secret information.

Ethical hacking includes five processes: Reconnaissance, Scanning, Gaining Access, Maintaining Access, and Covering tracks.

Phase 1	Reconnaissance
Phase 2	Scanning
Phase 3	Gaining Access
Phase 4	Maintaining Access
Phase 5	Clearing Track

Five Phases of Ethical Hacking

Phase 1:

Reconnaissance is a preparatory phase where the attacker collects information about the target. The target could be Organizations employees, clients, networks, or systems. There are two types of surveys: active surveillance and passive reconnaissance. Active management involves interacting with targets directly, like live telephone calls or help desk. Passive reconnaissance involves acquiring information without directly interacting with the target, like searching public records or news releases.

Phase 2:

Scanning is a pre-attack phase when an attacker scans the network for information based on information gathered during the first phase, i.e., surveillance. Scanning can include device names, operating systems, software installed on the course, IP addresses, port scanners, ping tools, network mappers, and accounts that exist. Attackers also extract information such as port status, OS details, live machines, system uptime, etc., to launch attacks.

Phase 3:

Gaining access is a point where the attacker gains access to the target system. The vulnerabilities exposed through phase 1 and phase 2 can now gain access to the target system. Gaining access is the third phase where hacking occurs, and the attacker can gain access at the operating system level, application level, or network level. The goal here is to obtain complete control of the system; attacks like password attack, Denial-of-service, session hijacking, etc., could be implemented by the attackers.

Phase 4:

Maintaining access is a phase where the attacker, after gaining access, would like to retain ownership of the system. Attackers could use tools like backdoors, trojans, rootkits, or any malicious software to continue to maintain their license to access and control the system. Attackers can also manipulate data, applications, and configurations on the network to maintain access and launch further attacks.

Phase 5:

Clearing track or covering track is a crucial phase to hide identity and avoid detection by defensive security. This phase involves removing any evidence of the attack by deleting event logs, erasing command history, using ICMP tunnearpl, reverse HTTP shells, etc. The attacker could overwrite the server, system, and application records to avoid suspicion. Covering tracks helps them to continue to have access to the victim's system while they remain unnoticed; otherwise, which might lead to the attacker's prosecution.

Ethical Hacking and Penetration Testing

Ethical hacking is hacking legally or with permission from the system owners. It gives ethical hackers the freedom to use whatever attack methods they have at their disposal to identify vulnerabilities. Ethical hackers are often hired by organizations before a new system goes live or if any significant updates are going live. This is predominantly done before testing the systems, identifying the weaknesses that can be exploited, documenting the findings, and preventing data theft due to attacks. Organizations call on ethical hackers as part of the 'bug bounty scheme, which offers financial rewards to hackers who identify and provide evidence of an exploitable flaw in the Organization's system. This is also one way to encourage talent and incentivize hackers to stay on the right side of the law. Well-known companies like Intel, Microsoft, Cisco, Apple, Snapchat, Google, Facebook, etc., offer bug bounty programs to encourage and recognize the skills of hacking enthusiasts.

Penetration testing or pen testing is a specific type of ethical hacking where organizations hire certified hackers to assess their cybersecurity defenses' strength. Pen testing is the practice of testing a computer system, a network, or web application to find security vulnerability that an attacker could exploit. The Client and the pen tester listed rules of engagement to ensure what is being tested, when it's being tried, and how it's being tested. There are three forms or types of pen testing:

White box testing is a software testing method that tests internal structures/design/ implementation of the item being tested is known to the security tester. This type of testing is typically done internally or by teams that perform internal audits of the system. Testers are provided with complete information about the target system, and this testing is design-driven testing. White box testing is also called structural box testing, precise box testing or transparent box testing, or glass box testing.

Black box testing is a software testing method in which the test's internal structure/ design/implementation is unknown to the tester. Black box testing will usually spend more time gathering information as testers are not given complete information about the target system. Black box testing is functional testing and can be referred to as outer or external software testing.

Gray box testing is a combination of white-box testing and black-box testing. Information given to the testing party is limited; gray box testing has been described as a partial-knowledge test.

The CIA Triad is a widely used information security model designed to guide information security policies within an organization. The universally agreed security triad of confidentiality, integrity, and availability (CIA) forms the basic building blocks of any good security initiative. Confidentiality addresses the secrecy and privacy of information. The core principle here is to safeguard sensitive information from unauthorized access attempts. Sensitive information in the wrong hands could result in fraud, identity theft, and financial loss. Integrity refers to methods and actions taken to protect sensitive data from unauthorized access. The relevant individuals must cover integrity by keeping the information accurate, unaltered, and in its original form. Integrity must be protected during storage and transit. Availability is the third leg of the CIA triad, and it means that the information must be made available to legitimate users.

The CIA Triad

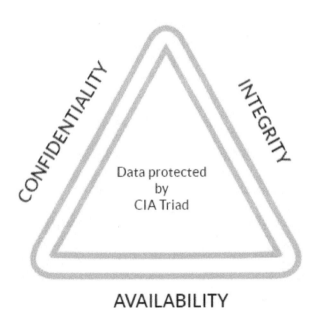

Incident Response (IR) is a process by which an organization handles a data breach or cyberattack, managing the consequences of the breach or attack and how the Organization responds to the attack or breach. Security incidents can happen without warning and are often undetected for an extended period. Organizations have overwhelming alerts, and security teams have been burdened with false signals, and it isn't straightforward to identify incidents impacting an organization's effectiveness with incident response. The Organization follows five stages of incident response to safeguard the Organization from a potential loss of data, information, or revenue.

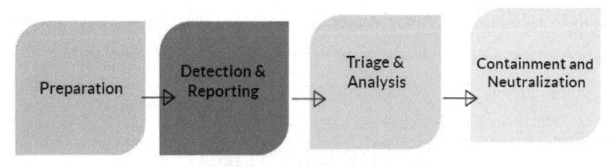

Incident Response Steps

Preparation: It is an efficient step to predetermined guidelines, as the response to the incident cannot be addressed without pre-planned and proposed guidelines. Some of the preparation step guidelines are developing and documenting IR policies, which establishes policies, procedures, and agreements for IR management. Defining communication guidelines creates communication standards and guidelines for uninterrupted and seamless communication during and after the incident. Incorporate threat intelligence feeds to perform ongoing collection, analysis, and synchronization of threat intelligence feed. It is conducting cyber hunting exercises to find incidents occurring within the environment. The final step of assessing the threat detection capability needs to set current threat detection capability and update risk assessment and improvement programs.

Detecting and Reporting: Incident detection is threat and attack detection. The focus of this phase is to monitor the threat and detect the intruders and the potential security incident by correlating alerts within a SIEM solution. Security analysts create an incident ticket, document all the initial findings, and assign an initial incident classification. Incident classification is a framework that appropriately prioritizes the incidents, helping develop meaningful metrics for future remediation. The first level of incident classification focuses on classifying the incident at the highest level, which details the category, type, and severity of the incident. E.g., the variety of the incident could be due to Malware or DOS. The kind of attack could be a state-sponsored act of Espionage or Insider threat, and the severity level could be a critical impact which is a threat to public safety or life. The second framework is incident taxonomy, which further dissects and focuses on detailing additional information about the security incident, identifying the root cause, and the security event trends. Reporting security events is an essential process of writing the security events to the proper authorities and accommodating regulatory reporting escalations.

Triage and Analysis: Triage is the first post-detection incident response process that the responder executes to open an incident or false security alerts. Monitoring and identifying compromise indicators (IoC) are critical for organizations to detect attacks and act quickly to prevent breaches from occurring or limit damages by stopping attacks in the initial stages. IoCs could be simple as metadata elements or incredibly complex malicious codes and are not always easy to detect. They are the red flags that indicate a potential or in-progress attack that could lead to systems compromise. Security analysts should have in-depth skills and a detailed understanding of live system responses, malware analysis, memory analysis, and digital forensics. Analysts should focus on in-depth and meticulous analysis after data collection; once the evidence is collected, analysts should focus on endpoint analysis, binary analysis, and enterprise analysis. Endpoint analysis (EPA) captures RAM (Random Access Memory) to analyze, parse and identify key artifacts to determine what occurred on a device. It gathers the artifacts needed to build a timeline of activities and defines the tracks that the threat actor could have left behind. RAM data is fundamental in a digital forensic investigation that starts with computer triage. Depending on the situation and the agency's policies and procedures, the investigators developed a plan to collect helpful evidence. The process of using these techniques and programs to collect, diagnose and analyze proper digital evidence, once the fault has been found, it is determined which course of action is taken based on the severity and importance.

This process of assigning a degree of urgency to take action is computer triage. The binary analysis investigates malicious binary tools leveraged by the attacker documenting the functionalities of those programs. Binary analysis is performed in two ways, i.e., behavioral analysis and static analysis. Behavioral analysis is the process of detecting the behavior of network anomalies; network behavior analysis (NBA) monitors traffic and notes the unusual actions on the standard network. NBA also helps in exploring the use of frequency, protocol, and methodologies to uncover events associated with multiple threat actors' intrusions into a simulated enterprise network. Static analysis is reverse engineering a malicious software program to scope out complete functionality. Reverse engineering is breaking the software code to discover the technological principles of the code or system through analysis of its pattern, structure, function, and operation to fix the errors in the software code. This could include activities like hidden code extraction, detecting and analyzing malware hooking behavior. Enterprise hunting is an analysis of existing systems and event log technologies to determine the scope of compromise. It's important to document all compromised accounts, systems, etc., for effective containment and Neutralization.

Containment and Neutralization

The response phase or containment of incident response is when the incident response team begins interacting with affected systems and attempts to keep further damage from occurring due to the incident.

Neutralization is one of the most crucial phases of the incident response process, which requires the intelligence gathered throughout the previous stages. Once all the systems and devices impacted by the breach have been identified, an organization performs a coordinated shutdown. To ensure that all employees are aware of the shutdown, employers send out notifications to all the IT team members. The next step is the infected systems and devices are wiped, clean, and rebuilt. Passwords on all accounts are also changed for security purposes. If any business discovers that there are domains or IP addresses that have been affected, it is essential to block all communication that could pose a risk.

Recovery

The recovery phase of an incident response plan involves restoring all affected systems and devices to allow for normal operations to continue. However, before getting all the systems back up and running, it is vital to ensure that the cause of the breach has been identified to prevent another breach from occurring again. During this phase, it's essential to consider the time required for normal operations to resume; it's essential to check the systems being patched and tested, it's also imperative to check if the system can be safely restored using a backup and the time needed for the system to be monitored.

Review

The final step in an incident response plan occurs after the incident has been solved. Throughout the adventure, all details should be documented to perfection so that the information can be used to prevent similar breaches in the future. All businesses should complete a detailed incident report that suggests tips on improving the existing incident plan. Companies should also closely monitor any post-incident activities to look for threats. It is crucial to coordinate across all departments of an organization so that all employees are involved and can do their part to help prevent future security incidents.

Post-Incident activity

This phase is often referred to as postmortem, where we determine specifically what happened, why it happened, and what we can do to prevent such incidents from happening again. Policies and infrastructure need to be changed accordingly to avoid such incidents happening again. Some of the top incident response service providers are Cygnet, FireEye Mandiant, SecureWorks, Signina, BAE Systems, AT&T Business, NTT Data, Trustwave, and Verizon.

Chain of custody

Chain of custody is a logical sequence that records custody, control, transfer, analysis, and disposition of physical or electronic evidence in criminal or legal cases. Each step in the chain is essential; if broken, then the evidence may be rendered inadmissible. Quality of evidence can be ensured when the chain of custody is preserved; this can be done by following the correct and consistent procedures. Let's discuss stages of the chain of custody:

Data collection: This is where the chain of custody process is initiated; it is the acquisition of data from all possible relevant sources that preserve the integrity of the data and evidence collected.

Examination: In this process, the chain of custody information is documented. It's important to capture the sequence and screenshots throughout the process to show the completed tasks and the evidence uncovered.

Analysis: This is the stage where you get the results; in this analysis stage, legally justifiable methods and techniques are used to derive useful information to address the problem or the case.

Reporting: Reporting includes statements regarding the chain of custody, explanation of tools used, description of various sources used for analysis, the issues and vulnerabilities identified, and recommendations for forensic measures that can be taken.

A Business Continuity Plan (BCP)

A business continuity plan refers to an organization system to restore critical business functions in an unplanned disaster. A business continuity plan (BCP) is a plan of action, and it ensures that regular business will continue even during a disaster. A BCP is designed to ensure that vital systems, services, and documents that support the business remain available to critical stakeholders and recover assets even when the bulk of critical systems are down. A disaster recovery plan (DRP) is a policy or process designed to assist an organization in executing recovery processes in response to a disaster to protect business and IT infrastructure and promote recovery.

March 2018 Sam Sam group - Ransomware attack on the city of Atlanta. The attack devastated the city government's computer systems, shutting down for five days and disrupting numerous city services, including police records, parking services, utilities, and other programs. Many departments were forced to complete essential paperwork by hand. Services were slowly brought back online, but full recovery of services and day-to-day operations took months. Attackers demanded a $51,000 Bitcoin equivalent ransom payment.

Chapter 4
Computer System Fundamentals

An important factor in computer system setup is whether the system is a standalone system or multiuser system connected to a host or a network and depends on them. A standalone system is a system that operates independently and is not related to any server or host system, unlike grid-connected systems. The standalone system performs tasks without being connected to any external systems or network. More than one person can use multiuser systems, and multiple users can access one single system; different users are connected to varying terminals through a network. A network is a system with computers connected to other computers. In a network with many users, one person is usually assigned to manage the computers' operation. This person is called a system administrator who takes care of the system right from starting up the computer system to shutting down the computer system. All related tasks like connecting terminals, printers, disks, tapes, modems, backing up files, getting new users started, protecting the system from unauthorized access.

IT is one main computer called the host computer, in a multiuser system connected and shared by all other computers. A host computer is a primary computer that controls all other computers. To be able to use any computer system, the host computer needs to be functional and start a session. To create a session, you need to log into the system. The main terminal connected to the host is called console, and the system administrator uses the console to manage the system. Within a network, every computer or a device connected to the network is called a node, and every node in a system has its unique address called MAC address. In a network, computers play one of two roles: server or Client. Sometimes a computer can play a dual role by acting as a client to one computer and server. A client is a program or machine that sends requests to servers, and a server is a program or device that waits for incoming requests and handles the request by providing services.

Network devices

Hub is a physical layer networking device that has been used to connect multiple devices in a network. They are used to connect computers in a Local area network (LAN). Hub has many ports, and computer systems are connected to the network through one of these ports. When the data frame arrives at a port, it is broadcasted to every other port. All systems connected to a hub share the same collision domain; therefore, every system on the corner receives the same data every other system on the seat sends or receives.

The switch is a data link layer device that resembles a hub switch and has many ports to which computers are plugged in. When a data frame arrives at any port of a network switch, it examines the determined destination address and sends the frame to the corresponding devices. Switches split collision domains, so each system connected to the switch resides in its collision domain, and thus it allows both unicast and multicast communications. Unlike a hub, the switch is an intelligent network device that uses packet switching to send and receive data over the network.

The switch can perform error checking before forwarding data and efficiently forward only good boxes selectively to correct ports. The router is a network layer device used to connect multiple devices to the Internet and connect them. Routers are also used to create local networks of devices connecting local area networks (LANs) and wide-area networks (WANs); they have dynamically updating routing tables. They make decisions on routing the data packets based on their IP addresses. Bridge operates at the data link layer, creating a single aggregate network from multiple communication networks. Routing allows various networks to communicate independently and yet remain separate, whereas a bridge connects two different networks as if they were a single network. A bridge is used to divide overburdened networks into smaller segments to ensure better bandwidth and traffic control use. When frames arrive at a bridge, the bridge determines whether or not the MAC address is on the local network segment. If the MAC address is not on the local network segment, the bridge forwards the frame to the necessary network segment.

Gateways can operate at any network level. As the name suggests, it acts as a gate between two networks or two different environments. When one domain uses a specific protocol and the other environment does not understand it, the gateway acts as a translator. The gateway can accept mail from one type of mail server and format it. A different mail server understands it by translating Internetwork packet exchange (IPX) protocol packets to IP packets.

The modem is a modulator and demodulator that modulates and demodulates electrical signals, and it transforms digital information from computers to analog signals that can transmit over wires. The modem is also a translator where it takes the cues from Internet Service Provider (ISP) and translates that to an internet connection for the Wi-Fi router to broadcast, giving access to the Web. Wi-Fi routers cannot communicate with ISP directly. They transmit different digital signal types but can only push the signals to the connected devices once the modem translates the digital signals received from ISP through optical fiber or coaxial cable.

The repeater is an electronic device operating at the physical layer. It receives digital signals and retransmits them. Repeaters are used to extend transmission length to cover longer distances and develop on the other side of an obstruction.

Access Point is a networking device within LAN that allows wireless-capable devices to connect to a wired network, creating a wireless local area network or WLAN in offices or large buildings. When there is no router within range on the other side of a colossal building, you can install an access point on the other side of the building and run an Ethernet cable or data cable to the broadband router or network switch.

An operating system is system software that manages computer hardware, software resources and provides standard services for computer programs. Some of the popular Desktop/ Laptop Operating Systems (OS) are Microsoft's Windows, Apple's Mac, Google's Chrome, Linux, Android, etc. Microsoft's Windows OS is leading the Desktop market share as of January 2021 (Source- Stat Counter) with 76.56%, where Windows 10 OS is the majority shareholder with a desktop/laptop share of 75.68%.

Network security is the process of taking preventive measures to protect the network infrastructure and data stored from unauthorized access and creating a secured platform for computers, users, and programs. Some of the network security devices and tools are Antivirus software, Firewalls, Application security, Email Security, Web security, Network segmentation, Security information, and event management, Mobile device security, Distributed Denial of Service prevention (DDoS), Data loss prevention (DLP), Behavioral analytics, Access control, etc.

Antivirus software is used to prevent, scan, detect and delete malicious software and viruses from computers; they also monitor the network traffic in real-time for Malware and offer threat remediation capabilities.

A firewall is a gatekeeper between a network and the Internet; they filter incoming and sometimes outgoing traffic. A firewall is designed to prevent unauthorized access to or from a private network. Firewalls can be implemented either in hardware or software form. The firewall also prevents unauthorized internet users from accessing private networks connected to the Internet and intranet.

Application security is making apps more secure by finding, fixing, and enhancing the security of apps. Some of the application security features include logging, authentication, authorization, encryption, and testing.

Email security is a terminology used to describe the procedures and techniques for protecting email accounts, email content, and communication against unauthorized access, loss, or compromise. Threat vectors like phishing attacks, suspicious links, and scams can be attached to the emails, affecting the system and could be a reason for data loss.

Web security also means Cybersecurity, and it means protecting a website or web application by detecting, preventing, and responding to cyber threats. There are few cybersecurity trends that everyone needs to watch out for:

- Social engineering attacks.

- Attacks on known and unknown internet-facing vulnerabilities.

- The exploitation of system administration and penetration tools.

- Ransomware attacks.

- Lack of automated monitoring tools.

Network segmentation

Here is what we know of network segmentation and the workings of it. What segmentation means in a layman's term is to divide into smaller parts. In computer terms, it means dividing a computer network into smaller pieces. This is done to improve the security of each network and its performance. Why does this work, you may ask? Well, it works by controlling how traffic flows among various parts. It's up to you to choose whether or not you want to stop all the traffic in one aspect from reaching another, or you can choose to limit the traffic flow by the type of traffic coming in, designation, source, etc. This determines your segmentation policy, how you choose to deal with the traffic.

To understand this concept further, let's consider an example. Think of a company with various branches. The company's policy has a restriction on branch heads from accessing its financial reporting system. Network segmentation can enforce the security policy by preventing all branch traffic from reaching the financial system. And by reducing overall network traffic, the financial system will work better for the financial analysts who use it.

If we consider today's technology, it simplifies segmentation by grouping and tagging network traffic. It then uses traffic tags to enforce segmentation policy directly on the network equipment, yet without the complexity of traditional approaches. You might have heard of the term micro- segmentation. What micro-segmentation does is that it uses much more information in segmentation policies like application-layer information. It enables policies that are more granular and flexible to meet the particular needs or business application.

Security information and event management

Security information and event management, or SIEM as we call it. has lasted for more than a decade now. Itof is software that allows enterprise security professionals to keep track of both in sight and a track record of the activitieswhat's happening within the IT environment.

The SIEM technology evolved from the log management discipline. It combines security event management (SEM) and security information management (SIM). The former helps analyze log and event data in real-time, whereas the latter gathers and analyzes information. SEM helps in event correlation, threat monitoring, and incident response, while SIM provides reports on log data.

SIEM gathers but also aggregates the log data that's acquired through the firm's technology infrastructure. This includes host systems and applications to the network, host systems, security devices such as antivirus filters and firewalls. The software helps in identifying, categorizing, and analyzing events and incidents. It acts on the following two major objectives:

- It s reports on all security-related incidents and events and incidents that vary from all kinds of malware activities to failed and successful, such as successful and failed logins, malware activity, other malicious activities.

- It sends alerts if the analysis shows that an activity is not going according to the rules set previously and points out potential security issues.

Paula Musich, research director at Enterprise Management Associates (EMA), has said that this technology was adopted earlier because the businesses needed better compliance management.

Mobile Device Security

This particular aspect refers to the same protection of secretive information and data saved and sent by any digital devices in your use. It is essential so that your information would not fall into the wrong hands or get leaked or misused by hackers.

These threats are particularly targeted and potentially harmful towards electronic and digital devices through mobile applications, scams, leaking data, badly secured Wi-Fi networks, amongst others. Moreover, companies have to keep in mind the possibility of employees losing the said device in question. Theft of the device also needs to be held into consideration. Most companies do, as they should, take measures to keep these mishaps in control to keep the risk at bay.

Distributed Denial of Service Prevention (DDoS)

A Denial of Service (DoS) attack is a malicious attempt to affect a targeted system's availability, such as a website or application, to legitimate end-users. Typically, attackers generate large volumes of packets or requests, ultimately overwhelming the target system. In the case of a Distributed Denial of Service (DDoS) attack, the attacker uses multiple compromised or controlled sources to generate the attack. In general, DDoS attacks can be segregated, by which the layer of the Open Systems Interconnection (OSI) model attacks.

Data loss prevention (DLP)

What do we grasp of the concept of data loss prevention? Let us talk of it in layman's terms, so you get the idea of what we are talking about. DLP is a set of tools and processes used so that sensitive data does not get lost, misused, or accessed by someone unwanted.

DLP software classifies regulated, confidential, and business-critical data and identifies violations of policies defined by organizations or within a predefined policy pack, typically driven by regulatory compliance such as HIPAA, PCI-DSS, or GDPR. Once the violations have been verified, DLP enforces remediation by sending alerts, **encryption**, and other protective actions to prevent end-users from accidentally or maliciously sharing data that could put the entire firm in some threat.

More so, data loss prevention software and tools monitor and control endpoint activities, filter data streams on corporate networks, and survey data in the cloud to protect data **at rest, in motion**, and use. DLP also provides reporting to meet compliance and auditing requirements and alert us about areas of weakness and anomalies for forensics and **incident response**.

User and Entity Behaviour Analytics (UEBA) is a form of cyber protection mechanism that tracks users' everyday actions. As a result, they spot some unusual behavior or occasions where the "normal" patterns are broken. For example, if a user routinely downloads 10 MB of files per day but then unexpectedly downloads gigabytes of files, the device will be able to notice this phenomenon and notify them right away. UEBA uses machine learning, algorithms, and mathematical analysis to determine whether there is a divergence from known norms, indicating which of these deviations could pose a natural hazard. UEBA may also aggregate data from reports and documents and interpret data from folders, flows, and packets.

You don't log security incidents or control systems in UEBA; instead, you track all of the system's users and organizations. As a result, UEBA focuses on internal risks, such as rogue workers, corrupted employees, and individuals that already have access to your infrastructure and then carry out targeted hacks and fraud attempts, as well as computers, software, and computers that are operating inside your system. It also helps you to spot attacks, hacked passwords, access updates, and data breaches.

In a nutshell, UEBA is needed to keep a firm check on any organization's internal workings, leaving little to no room for risks as it keeps track of who uses the organization's system. It is a more comprehensive way to ensure your security is up to the set standard while providing help with detecting users that might compromise the organization's entire system.

Access control

Access management is a technique for ensuring that customers think they are and have proper access to organization information. In the most basic form, access control is the selective limitation of data access. According to Daniel Crowley, head of research for IBM's X- Force Red, which focuses on data protection, it consists of two key components: authentication and authorization.

Authentication is a method of ensuring that someone is who they say they are. Crowley points out that authentication isn›t enough to keep data secure. An additional layer, permission, is necessary to decide if a user should be authorized to access data or complete the transaction they are attempting.

Network topologies

Network topology is a basic layout of the network. It consists of two parts, the physical part, and the logical part. The physical part describes the physical structure, while the rational part describes how the data flows in that network. Both physical and logical parts are also known as the physical topology and the logical topology.

There are different types of topologies, for example, bus topology, star topology, hybrid topology, ring topology, mesh topology, and point-to-point topology.

OSI model

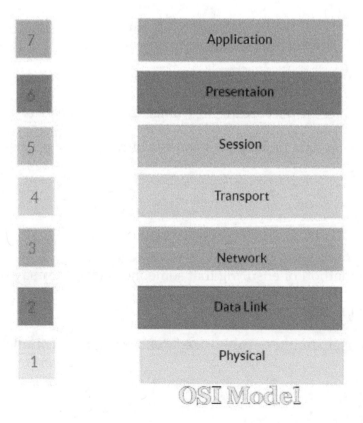

The OSI Model (Open Systems Interconnection Model) is a conceptual framework used to describe a networking system's functions. The OSI model characterizes computing functions into a universal set of rules and requirements to support interoperability between different products and software. The communications between a computing system are split into seven different abstraction layers in the OSI reference model. These layers are the Physical, Data Link, Network, Transport, Session, Presentation, and Application.

Created at a time when network computing was in its infancy, the OSI was published in 1984 by the International Organization for Standardization (ISO). Though it does not always map directly to specific systems, the OSI Model is still used today to describe Network Architecture.

There are seven different layers involved in this. Physical Layer, Data Link Layer, Network Layer, Transport Layer, Session Layer, Presentation Layer, and Application Layer. **TCP/IP and ports** IP Subnetting is the subdivision of IP addresses into two or more networks; the logical subdivision of IP addresses into two fields are the network number and host identifier.

Internet Protocol address (IP address) is a unique number assigned to each device connected to a computer network that uses that Internet Protocol for communication. An IP address identifies the location of the computer on the Internet and the internet service provider. The practice of dividing a network into two or more networks is called subnetting. A subnet or subnetwork is a logical subdivision of an IP network into two fields: the network number or routing prefix and the host identifier. The goal of subnetting is to create a fast, efficient and resilient computer network. An engineer can create smaller mini-routes within a more extensive network to allow traffic to travel efficiently and the shortest route, avoiding congestion and bottlenecks. Subnetting divides broadcast domains and limits the IP address used within a few devices, Hexadecimal, and binary conversion.

The hexadecimal numeral system is made up of 16 symbols (base16). The standard numeral system is called decimal (base 10) and uses ten symbols: 0,1,2,3,4,5,6,7,8,9. While Hexadecimal uses the decimal numbers and six extra symbols. Binary (base -2) is a numeric system that uses just two digits - 0 and 1. Computers operate in binary, storing all data in zeros and ones. Computers use voltages and voltages often, and no specific voltage is set for each number in the decimal system. Binary is measured as a two-state system, i.e., ON or OFF, making it easier for the computer to operate in a binary system, which also helps keep the calculations simple. In other words, computers don't understand words or numbers like humans do. To make sense of complex data, computers have to encode it in binary using 0s and 1s, which corresponds to ON and OFF states that the computer understands. Bits and bytes play a major role in binary systems. The byte is the smallest addressable unit of memory in many computer architectures. The byte is a digital information unit or data size consisting of eight bits, so these 8 bits are used to encode a single text character in a computer. Conversion of Hexadecimal to binary and vice versa is compact and convenient to represent byte values, i.e., numbers from 0 to 255.

Domain Name System (DNS) is an essential component of the Internet's functionality since the mid-1980s. DNS is something like a telephone directory of the Internet. It translates human-friendly computer hostnames or domain names into numerical IP addresses and directs the internet traffic to the right website. DNS provides a worldwide distributed directory service mapping hostnames to IP addresses. For example, www.eccouncil.org is the hostname or a domain name; when you look up the IP address, it gives out 104.18.21.251.

Proxies and firewalls work towards a common goal, limiting or blocking connections to or from a network. Firewall blocks access to unauthorized connections while proxy server sits as a mediator between local computer and Internet to retrieve data on behalf of a user.

Intrusion Prevention System (IPS) and Intrusion Detection System (IDS)

An intrusion prevention system (IPS) continuously monitors the network looking for possible malicious incidents and captures information about them protects it from abuse and attack. IPS is a form of network security that scans real-time network traffic, detects and prevents identified threats. IPS is proactive and preventive, and it takes steps to prevent further damage and thwart another attack.

Intrusion Detection Systems (IDS) monitors the network for potential threats, sends alerts to the system administrators, and is not designed to block attacks. IDS is passive and does not take any preventive action to stop the attack.

Media Access Control (MAC) address is a unique identification number or code that ensures the computer's physical address or hardware address. Whether the network is wired or wireless takes both network software and hardware like cables, routers, etc., to transfer data from your computer to another. MAC address is a string of six sets of two digits or characters separated by colons. For example, when you open the windows command prompt and type ipconfig/all, you will see MAC address as Physical Address. . . . .: B8-81-98-5C-CB-7C. Here B8-81-98 identifies the Intel Corporate manufacturer and is also called OUI (Organizational Unique Identifier).

Chapter 5
Sniffers and Sniffing

Sniffers are data interception technology, and they are utilities used to capture and scan traffic moving across a network. Sniffers examine streams of data packets that flow between computers on a target network, monitoring and capturing all the data packets passing through the target network. Sniffing is a process of monitoring and capturing all data packets passing through a given network using sniffing tools. There are two broad categories of Packet Sniffers: Hardware Packet Sniffers and Software Packet Sniffers. A sniffer can be a software or hardware tool that allows the user to sniff or monitor internet traffic in real-time, capturing all the data flowing to and from your computer. Hackers use Sniffers to capture data packets containing sensitive information such as login information, password, account information, etc. A malicious intruder can place a sniffer on a promiscuous network to capture and analyze network traffic.

ZERO DAY VULNERABILITY

Five phases of of Zero day exploit cycle :
1. Vulnerability
2. Identify the target
3. Target Breached
4. Vendor works to fix software
5. Vendor releases the patch

Sniffing occurs in the Data Link Layer of the OSI Model; an attacker can sniff sensitive information from a network. Some of the protocols that are vulnerable to sniffing attacks include:

Web traffic - Hypertext Transfer Protocol (HTTP)

Email traffic - Simple Mail Transfer Protocol (SMTP), Post Office Protocol (POP), Internet Message Access Protocol (IMAP)

File Transfer Protocol (FTP) traffic - Telnet authentication, FTP Passwords, Server Message Block (SMB), Network File System (NFS), and many more.

Some of the popular Network Sniffing tools: Wireshark, SolarWinds Network Packet Sniffer, Tcpdump, Windpump, ManageEngine, Network Miner, Cola soft Capsa, Telerik Fiddler, Kismet, NetFlow Analyzers, Omni Peek, Sniff, Ether Ape, MSN Sniffer, Net Witness NextGen, PRTG Network Monitor are some of the recommended network sniffing tools.

Media Access Control (MAC) attack or MAC flooding is a method intended to compromise the network switches' security. Content Addressable Memory table (CAM table) is a MAC table that consists of individual MAC addresses of the host computers on the network connected to ports of the switch. Switches maintain these MAC tables on the web to the physical ports on a button.

The Dynamic Host Configuration Protocol (DHCP) is a network management protocol used on Internet Protocol (IP) local area networks. The primary function of DHCP is to assign

IP addresses, default gateways, and other network parameters to client devices. The DHCP server controls a range of IP addresses and allocates them to clients permanently or for a defined period. Permanent or Static IP is where users manually type in an IP address, Subnet mask, and default gateway. Dynamic IP is where a computer gets an IP address from a DHCP server. A DHCP server automatically assigns an IP address, subnet mask, default gateway, and DNS server. DHCP spoofing attack occurs when an attacker attempts to respond to DHCP requests and list themselves as the default gateway or DNS server initiating a man-in-the-middle (MITM) attack.

ARP Poisoning

It is also referred to as spoofing for the same kind. Cybercrimes happen over a LAN that includes sending baleful ARP packets to a certain set gateway on a LAN to shake the pairing in its IP to MAC address table. ARP Protocol translates IP addresses into MAC addresses. These attacks are simpler to carry out because of the fact that the ARP protocols and entente were created to make sure of efficiency instead of security. However, they are only simpler as long as the attacker can take charge of the machine within the target or directly have a connection with it.

The attack contains traces of an attacker found sending incorrect ARP replies to the standard network pathway. It also informs it that the MAC address must be associated with their target's dress. The attack itself consists of an attacker sending a false ARP reply message to the default network gateway, informing it that their MAC address should be associated with their target's dress. It also works the other way around. At the point that the standard gateway has attained the message and it ends up broadcasting its changes to every other device on the network, all the targets to all other devices on the web travel across the attacker, giving the attacker the leverage to inspect or make a change to it before sending it forth to its actual destination. Since ARP poisoning attacks happen on a lower level, users often find themselves under threat. These users mostly do not comprehend that their traffic is being meddled with. Other than the Man-in-the-middle-attacks, ARP Poisoning can be utilized to cause an in-service denial condition over a LAN by basically interjecting and not putting the target forth.

In a few cases, we need to know that ARP can compromise your security. ARP spoofing, or ARP poisoning, is a process used by an attacker to inject the wrong MAC address association into a network by issuing fake ARP requests.

Spoofing Attack

Lately, fraudsters are combining age-old deception methods with modern technology to create brand new attacks. A spoofing attack is a cyberattack that occurs when a scammer disguises themselves as a trusted agency or source to gain access to sensitive information. Spoofing is an impersonation act and can happen through emails, phone calls, text messages, IP addresses, websites, and servers. Cybercriminals employ various methods and techniques to carry out spoofing attacks and steal their victim's sensitive information. Some common spoofing types include MAC spoofing, Email spoofing, DNS spoofing, IP spoofing, DDoS spoofing, GPS spoofing, and ARP spoofing. Media Access Control (MAC) attack or MAC flooding is a method intended to compromise the network switches' security. Content Addressable Memory table (CAM table) is a MAC table that consists of individual MAC addresses of the host computers on the network connected to ports of the switch. Switches maintain these MAC tables on the web to the physical ports on the switch. MAC spoofing attack is a technique for changing a factory - assigned unique MAC address of a network interface on a networked device. The MAC address that is hard-coded on a network interface controller (NIC) cannot be changed, but it can mask it on the software side. This masking is what is referred to as MAC spoofing. MAC spoofing attack is where the attacker sniffs the network for a valid MAC address and attempts to act as one of the correct MAC addresses. The attacker represents themselves as the default gateway and copies all the data forwarded to the default gateway. This provides valuable attacker information, details of the applications in use, and destination IP addresses. They can overwrite and spoof the CAM entry. Cisco certified expert well explains the three steps below:

Email spoofing is when an attacker sends emails with false sender addresses, part of a phishing scam. The sender forges email headers so that client software displays the fraudulent sender's address, showing that it came from a person or entity they either know or can trust.

This happens when another party imitates and copies the other device or user to launch different kinds of malicious attacks against network hosts, expand on spyware, commit data theft, or meddle with access controls by going through them. There isn't one but many different types and forms of these attacks that the attackers can use for this purpose.

IP address spoofing is one of the most frequently used spoofing attack methods. An attacker sends IP packets from a false source address to disguise itself in an IP address spoofing attack.

Denial-of-service attacks often use IP spoofing to overload networks and devices with packets that appear to be from legitimate source IP addresses.

There are two ways that IP spoofing attacks can be used to overload targets with traffic. One method is to flood a selected target with packets from multiple spoofed addresses. This method works by directly sending a victim more data than it can handle. The other process is spoofing the target's address and sending packets from that address to many different recipients on the network. When another machine receives a package, it will automatically transmit a packet to the sender in response. Since the spoofed packets appear to be sent from the target's address, all responses to the spoofed packets will be sent to (and flood) the target's address.

MAC spoofing

A MAC spoofing attack is where the intruder sniffs the network for valid MAC addresses and attempts to act as one of the correct MAC addresses. The intruder then presents itself as the default gateway and copies all of the data forwarded to the default gateway without being detected. This provides the intruder valuable details about applications in use and destination host IP addresses. This enables the spoofed CAM entry on the switch to be overwritten as well.

In conjunction with port security, the best method is to use DHCP snooping mechanisms to ensure that only valid DHCP servers are enabled across your network. One DHCP snooping mechanism permits only trusted DHCP messages to flow between client PC and authorized DHCP servers. The ideal solution to mitigate various ARP-based network exploits is DHCP snooping and Dynamic ARP Inspection (DAI).

When a client sends out a broadcast message for an IP address, the intruder sees the request, of course, because broadcasts are sent out to all interfaces or ports except the source port. In effect, the network must not allow DHCP offers, acknowledgments, or negative acknowledgments (DHCP offer, DHCP ack, or DHCP Nek) to be sent from untrusted sources.

Illegal DHCP messages are messages received from outside the network or firewall. The DHCP snooping binding table contains the MAC address, IP address, lease time, binding type, VLAN number, and interface information corresponding to the local untrusted interfaces; it does not, however, contain information regarding hosts interconnected with a trusted interface.

By configuring trusted and entrusted DHCP sources, the switch can be configured to drop illegal frames immediately. DHCP snooping will still not stop an intruder sniffing for MAC addresses.

DAI determines an ARP packet›s validity based on the valid MAC address—to—IP address bindings stored in a DHCP snooping database. This means that only valid MAC addresses are permitted to reply to authorize devices on the network. Some crafty attackers are out there waiting to pounce on networks, and for a majority of them, these features are not enabled, so it is a gold mine in many parts of the world, even in todays' age.

DNS Poisoning

To get an idea of what DNS poisoning is, we will talk about what DNS is. Understand DNS as a massive phone book that refers to IP addresses with assigned domain names. Your browser doesn't understand domain names – to retrieve a website, and it needs the server's IP address where it is hosted. When you enter a domain name, this DNS phone book finds the IP to connect to.

Now let us understand what DNS poisoning is. A DNS attack is a cyberattack in which the attacker exploits vulnerabilities in the Domain Name System. This is a grave issue in cybersecurity because the DNS system is a crucial part of the internet infrastructure, and at the same time, it has many security holes. Domain Name Server (DNS) Poisoning or spoofing is a cyber-attack that exploits system vulnerabilities in the domain name server to divert traffic away from legitimate servers and directs it towards fake ones. Altered DNS records are used to redirect online traffic to fraudulent websites that resemble the original webpage or destination. This redirection of traffic from real websites to fake websites by the attacker allows the attacker to steal data, spread malware, inject malicious software, etc.

IP spoofing occurs at the network level; it creates internet protocol (IP) packets with a false source IP address to impersonate another computing system. The data transmitted over the internet is first broken into multiple packages, and those packets are sent independently and reassembled at the end. Each packet has an IP (Internet Protocol) header that contains information about the packet, including the source IP address and the destination IP address. In IP spoofing, hackers use tools to modify the packet header's source address to make the receiving computer system think that the packet is from a trusted source on a legitimate network and accept it. This type of attack is common in Denial-of-service (DoS) attacks, which overwhelms computer network traffic, shutting them down. A man-in-the-middle attack is another IP spoofing method used to interrupt the communication between two computers, alter the packets and transmit them without the original sender or receiver being aware of this. In due course, hackers collect a wealth of confidential information they can use and sell.

There are many different ways in which DNS can be attacked. DNS reflection attacks, DoS, DDoS, and DNS poisoning are just some of the attack types DNS is susceptible to.

Now we understand that attackers are not super hackers that cannot be stopped. All they do is look for vulnerabilities in the DNS and attack them.

There are a few things we can do as users to mitigate attacks on DNS:

1. If you operate your DNS resolver, restrict the usage to only users connected to your network. This will help to prevent attackers from poisoning your resolver.

2. If you run your DNS server, then make sure you keep the DNS server and the OS they run patched and updated to prevent them from being exploited due to known vulnerabilities.

Distributed Denial of Service Prevention (DDoS)

Distributed denial-of-service attack or DDoS attack is a malicious attempt to disrupt a targeted server's regular traffic. It occurs when multiple systems are flooded with a targeted system's bandwidth or resources, usually one or more web servers. DDoS uses more than one unique IP address or machine, often from thousands of hosts infected with malware.

Global Positioning System (GPS) spoofing is an attack whose primary goal is to override a GPS-enabled device's original location. The attacker uses a radio transmitter that broadcasts a fake GPS signal and interferes with GPS receivers nearby. As a result, those devices display mock GPS locations. By downloading third-party apps, smartphones can spoof their GPS and fool other apps. GPS spoofing is used in Apps, warfare, taxi trips, construction disruption, geofencing, etc. Some Apps can help you spoof smartphone locations; this could help while playing games like Pokémon Go which has privacy issues. This Niantic's smartphone games like Pokémon Go turns the world into a playing board, it needs access to the camera to recreate the environment, it also needs location data to show where you are on the map, name, and email address for 'registration purposes' and tons of permissions and personal information that are uncalled for, giving the companies and the world access to all your personal information, GPS spoofing could be one of the solutions to protect your privacy and these GPS spoofers can mislead others about your perceived locations. GPS spoofing is a much-discussed cyber threat to modern military systems.

Spoofing can generate position and timing inaccuracies on a battlefield, resulting in a potential lead to the uselessness or usefulness of modern weapon systems. GPS spoofing is sometimes helpful in warfare to fake a war troop's location while attacking enemies. According to the latest analysis reports, GPS spoofing threats have increased after the Russian military intervention in Ukraine and Syria. Researchers have found out that Russia is using GPS spoofing technology in Russian-controlled areas of Syria. Taxi drivers can use GPS spoofing to fake their location to earn more money. GPS navigators are used to controlling some construction equipment and machinery. Equipment and machinery are the assets that construction companies seek to track as they are expensive and if it goes missing, would eat into their company's profits. Using GPS spoofing, a thief could move an asset to a new location without anyone knowing about it. GPS systems are also used to track delivery drivers and deliveries. Long-distance truck drivers have GPS-powered geofencing systems that lock this truck until it reaches its destination. Malicious actors can GPS-spoof the truck's location to steal its cargo.

ARP Poisoning or spoofing = (ARP) is a communication protocol used for discovering the link-layer address, such as MAC address, associated with a given internet layer address, typically an IPv4 address. This mapping is a critical function in the internet protocol suite. ARP Poisoning is a type of cyber-attack carried out over a local area network (LAN) that involves sending malicious ARP packets to a default gateway on a LAN to change the pairings in its IP to MAC address table. ARP protocol translates IP addresses into MAC addresses. ARP works between network layer two and layer 3 of the open systems interconnection model (OSI model). The MAC address exists on layer 2, the data link layer, and the IP address exists on layer 3, the network layer. ARP is a broadcast protocol, and it is a process of maliciously changing an ARP cache on a Machine to inject faulty entries, which is not a complicated process to achieve.

Countermeasures

The countermeasures taken under consideration for DNS poisoning or spoofing can look a bit like filtering your DNS servers. What it means is that not allowing DNS servers to answer on the internet over port 53. Even as you do this, the restricted aim of the attack vector is not entirely eliminated. You need to understand DNS's needs and consider using RNDC encryption, stub zones, and reducing TTL values on your internal DNS server(s). Commercial products, such as Infoblox will definitely do this for you. There are dozens of "DNS/D" CP Security" suit "s that make this task MUCH easier. But they are expensive, and not every person will be able to justify their cost.

Another thing you can do to ensure your safety is internal DNS security development. But to make it easier for you, here is a list of countermeasures you might be interested in going through

- Set up and maintain your DNS servers. It's not that hard. even for a small network. Windows or BIND DNS can be securely and properly be configured in no more than 30 minutes. Its MIT is better than the option of "hosted" DNS." Better to keep away from DNS requests over the WAN on port 53 (or any other port for that matter).

- You should use RNDC keys if you wish to answer on the 53rd port and rotate them often.

- The TTL's value should be set to a lower value, like 15 minutes, for instance. However, it shouldn't be at the cost of your network performance. For example, if a cache poison DOES affect you, the problem will last for only a little while.

- DEACTIVATE THE 'HOSTS' FILE 'RESOLUTION ON YOUR SERVERS AND ALSO YOUR CLIENTS!!!

- Design and properly maintain your PTR zones for local domains also. It's is EXTREMELY important, as far as SMTP traffic is concerned.

- Think about using the STUB zones for frequently accessed domains or easily compromised domains.

- Make use of DNS forwarders ONLY when you want to verify DNS servers. Most people just forward to the 'Root 'servers,' but this isn't right, and some don't answer. Note that you can end up making your poisoned cache with a localized routing table attack which is why you shouldn't talk. Only talk to your ISP, making use of their servers. Furthermore, frequently Investigate them using 'dig." Make sure that the DHCP is blocked on your firewall. Take note that if a problematic DHCP server is permitted to permeate your network, you lose will *all* control over your DNS and DHCP security. Know that it is very difficult and frustrating to track a problematic DHCP server.

- Learn how DNS works. Learn more than at the surface level (which I've covered a bit here), but at its core level as well. Once you do, you can see how some of the inherited flaws can be 'stopp'd' with your network structure.

- Collect the resources of your DNS. Many modern-day problems with DNS had resulted from the time when performance was terrible and computing resources were finite. However, this isn't the case anymore. This is because the TTLs that are shorter expand your database I/O. However, not in the way that your users will be notified. Make sure to do your tests. Eventually, you will most likely be a little shocked to see that having 'more' real-time outcomes isn't influencing your dormancy or I/O on your DNS infrastructure.

Sniffing detection techniques:

Detecting Sniffers: Ping method, ARP method, On Local Host, Latency Method, ARP Watch, Using IDS.

Preventing Sniffing:

The best way to secure against sniffing is to use encryption to ensure what the sniffer reads are junk.

Sniffing pen testing

A penetration test, also known as a pen test, simulates a malware attack on the operating system to find exploitable flaws. Penetration monitoring is sometimes used to supplement a web application firewall in the sense of web application reliability (WAF). Pen research involves trying to hack into a multitude of program frameworks in attempts to identify defects. There are certain advantages to pen tests: Vulnerabilities in the code should be identified and fixed via pen tests to understand the digital systems better and Build a relationship of confidence with the customers. Sniffing is the method of continuously tracking and recording all data packets that travel across a network. Network/system operators use sniffers to track and troubleshoot network traffic. Attackers use sniffers to intercept data packets containing personal data such as passwords and account records. Sniffers may be mounted as hardware or software in the device. A malicious attacker can intercept and interpret all network traffic by using a packet sniffer in promiscuous mode on a network. Now there are two types of sniffing, respectively:

1. **Active sniffing:** Active sniffing is sniffing in the switch. A switch is a network interface that connects two points. The controller monitors the flow of data between its ports by constantly checking the MAC address on each terminal, ensuring that data is only transmitted to the correct destination. To catch traffic between targets, sniffers must aggressively inject traffic into the LAN to allow traffic sniffing.

2. **Passive sniffing:** This is how you smell your way around the hub. Both devices on the segment can see all traffic that goes through the non-switched or unabridged network segment. Sniffers operate at the network's data link layer. Any data transmitted over the LAN is sent to every computer connecting to the network.

Mitigating MAC flooding

MAC stands for media access control. A media access control policy is a network data transmission policy that specifies how data is transferred over a network cable between two computer terminals. More than often, these come into attack, which is an act of cybercrime and is very dangerous when personal data is taken into consideration. This procedure is known as flooding, more specifically MAC flooding. In a standard MAC flooding attack, the attacker feeds a switch a large number of Ethernet frames, each with a separate source MAC address. There are ways to prevent such an act from taking place, which can better secure your network. First off, port protection is often used as a defense against MAC Flooding attacks. On ports attached to the end stations, the switches are designed to restrict the number of MAC addresses that can be learned. With the traditional MAC address table, a small table of 'secure' MAC addresses is also held. The MAC address table is also a subset of this table.

In certain situations, security steps to avoid ARP or IP spoofing can require different MAC address filtering on unicast packets. You can also try implementing IEEE suites to your network for added protection. Using IEEE 802.1X suites, a AAA server can directly install packet filtering rules based on dynamically learned knowledge about clients, such as the MAC address. Above this, another applicable countermeasure is to avoid regular unicast flooding for undisclosed MAC addresses; additional security mechanisms are also used and the above. This function usually relies on the "port safe" feature to keep all protected MAC addresses in the ARP table of layer three devices for at least as long as they stay in the ARP table. As a result, the aging period of acquired protected MAC addresses can be adjusted separately. These are some of the best measures you could use to mitigate media access control floorings.

Cisco IOS Mitigation

Weakness occurs in the Smart Install function of Cisco Catalyst Switches running the Cisco IOS Program, which may cause a remote intruder to execute code on the affected computer. Without authentication or end-user intervention, this flaw can be abused remotely. Exploitation is carried out through designed Smart Install packets sent over TCP port 4786. CVE-2011-3271 is the CVE code for this vulnerability. Administrators are recommended to install infrastructure access control lists (iACLs) to conduct policy enforcement of traffic sent to infrastructure equipment to secure infrastructure devices and reduce the risk, effects, and effectiveness of direct infrastructure attacks. Administrators may create an iACL by expressly allowing only approved traffic to be sent to infrastructure devices, as long as current security protocols and configurations are followed. Deployed iACLs should be deployed in the ingress direction on all interfaces on which an IP address has been configured for complete infrastructure system security. When the attack originates from a trusted source address, an iACL workaround cannot offer complete protection against these vulnerabilities. The iACL policy prohibits unwanted Smart Install packets from being sent to affected users over TCP port 4786. The affected devices' IP address space is 192.168.60.0/24 in the following case, and the host at 192.168.100.1 is called a trustworthy source that allows access to the affected devices. Before refusing all illegal traffic, make sure to enable relevant traffic for routing and administrative access. Infrastructure address space should be kept separate from the address space used by customer and utility segments wherever possible. The construction and implementation of iACLs can be aided by using this addressing technique.

NETGEAR Mitigation

NETGEAR is a respected establishment that is responsible for creating hardware products for business and other purposes. NETGEAR's offerings include a broad range of popular technologies, including wireless (Wi-Fi and LTE), Ethernet, and power line, emphasizing security and ease of use. For internet access and network communication, the items provide wired and wireless applications. For some time now, the products being produced at NETGEAR prove to be a handful due to various vulnerabilities popping up. Various SerComm- manufactured Net gear goods were discovered to have a loophole that permitted unauthorized remote access to the affected computers. Net gear and other firms with SerComm- manufactured products that were harmed by the backdoor, released software fixes for some of the affected devices. However, it was quickly discovered that the patches merely concealed the loophole rather than removing it. The vulnerability was discovered independently by two security experts, Adam Nichols of cyber-security firm GRIMM and d4rkn3ss of Vietnamese internet service provider VNPT. Because of the lack of adequate security measures, an attacker will craft malicious HTTP requests that can be used to gain control of the router. Nichols said he was able to "launch the [router's] telnet daemon as root listening on TCP port 8888 and not requiring a password to "login in a proof-of-concept exploit published on GitHub. As demonstrated by previous accidents, router vulnerabilities are becoming a rising security issue. Businesses and home consumers are now more vulnerable to attacks from hacked computers and unsecured routers as IoT devices become more widely adopted. Attackers aren't just attacking PCs anymore; they're still using routers as a viable way of obtaining victims' credentials. Due to the issues stated, NETGEAR has been on the ropes and is slowly declining when selling its products. As a result, the company's mitigation is a slow but sure process as newer and more secure alternatives are being offered, such as Linksys.

Detecting Sniffing attack.

Non-promiscuous mode and promiscuous mode are the two modes in which a sniffer can operate. Sniffers that function in the non-promiscuous mode will capture data from the network that is addressed to or transmitted from the sniffer's device. Promiscuous mode allows a network adapter to collect all network traffic data, regardless of the destination address, that passes through the network. Sniffers can catch all network traffic in promiscuous mode. Some methods that help with the detection of sniffers are as follows:

1. **Latency method:** The Latency System transfers a vast volume of data over the network and pins the suspect computer before and after floods. If the sniffer is operating on the server, it will be promiscuous, which means it will need to parse the data, putting more strain on the computer. Due to the high volume, responding to ping requests can take longer. This delay may mean the existence of a sniffer on the target system.

2. **Host monitoring:** In a busy network, collecting and processing large amounts of network data will strain the CPU. To save the collected network info, you'll need a lot of storage space. Increased CPU workload and disc used for no particular cause could suggest the existence of a sniffer on that computer.

3. **ARP method:** IP addresses are resolved to MAC addresses using the Address Resolution Protocol (ARP). Fixed addresses are stored in a computer's cache for future use. We give a non-broadcast ARP here. A laptop would cache your ARP address in promiscuous mode. Then, using our IP but a separate MAC address, we send a broadcast ping packet. Only the computer with the correct MAC address from the previous sniffed ARP frame will respond to the broadcast ping message.

Chapter 6
Social Engineering

Social Engineering is a nontechnical attack that involves human interaction. It is an art of exploiting human psychology to gain access to systems or sensitive information. Social engineering is all about manipulating individuals on an interpersonal level, and the hacker tries to gain victims and persuade them to reveal confidential and sensitive information. Social engineers trick or coerce victims to disclose information that violates everyday security practices. Once they gain the knowledge, they use it to carry out actions like identity theft or stealing passwords. They scam people by posing themselves as bank employees, system administrators, or technical support engineers to gain confidential and sensitive information required to make a social engineering attack.

Some of the techniques used for social engineering attacks are Phishing, watering, impersonation, pretexting, baiting, tailgating, quid pro quo. Phishing is a fraudulent practice of sending emails to induce individuals to reveal personal and confidential information like credit card details, passwords, or OTP. The attackers masquerade as a trusted entity to lure individuals into providing sensitive information.

Cyberwarfare is a digital attack used to attack a nation, causing harm and disrupting the vital computer system. A watering hole attack is a process of injecting malicious code into a website or into the web pages of a website that the target frequently visits. Once the target sees the compromised website or web page, a backdoor Trojan is installed. Eventually, members of the targeted group will become infected. A watering hole attack is widespread for a state-sponsored attack or cyber-espionage operation.

An Impersonation attack is an act of deceiving someone by pretending to be another person. It is a form of fraud in which attackers assume the identity of one of the legitimate parties in a system and pose as a known or trusted person to cheat the target person or target entity into sharing confidential information or transferring money to a fraudulent account.

Pretexting attack is a social engineering attack where the attacker creates a convincing and compelling story or a setting to fool individuals and businesses into disclosing sensitive information. It is nothing but psychological manipulation of people into divulging sensitive and confidential information.

Baiting attacks are made by luring users into a trap and inflicting their systems with Malware to steal their personal information. When an attacker intentionally leaves Malware infected USB drive in a conspicuous area where potential victims are sure to see them is baiting. Once the curious victim plugs the USB into the computer system, malicious software could be installed in the victims' system. Protesters use different techniques and tactics such as Impersonation, Phishing, vishing, tailgating to gain the targets, convincing victims to break their security policies, and give valuable information to attackers.

Tailgating or Piggybacking is a physical security breach where an unauthorized person is lurking around the secured and restricted entrance waiting for an opportunity to closely follow an authorized person to gain access into a secured and restricted facility.

Quid Pro Quo attack promises a benefit in exchange for information, and this benefit usually assumes the form of service. The most common scenario of 'quid Pro quo' attacks involves attackers who impersonate IT service people and spam call as many direct numbers that belong to a company as they can find; these attackers offer IT assistance to everyone their targets. The attacker promises a quick fix in exchange for the victim disabling their Antivirus software on the computer and installing a new version of the software, including Malware on their computers that assumes the guise of a software update. The fraudster can also offer services to solve computer issues in return for victims' credentials.

Power of social engineering

We grab by the concept of social engineering is how powerful human hacking can get given the ever-advancing technology; our data is constantly exposed to getting hacked if proper measures are not taken. It uses extraordinary ways to trick people into revealing their essential information to the wrong people.

With technology constantly getting more sophisticated and complex, it is the human element in organizations seen as the easiest target to go after. So rather than trying to disable all security cameras and open the heavily guarded safe door using the most innovative and expensive gear, the hacker will use psychological methods to get the teller to practically hand over the gold bars.

In a broad range, social engineering is the term used for malicious activities accomplished through human interactions. It is psychological manipulation to trick users into making security mistakes or giving away sensitive information. The attacker first investigates the targeted victim to gather necessary information about the victim›s background information, personal information, financial information, etc.

This hacking does for the people because they can use your private information to steal your identity or blackmail you for money, or could sell your information to a third party to get a handsome price for it. This could also be done to take a kick at you by leaking your sensitive data for the whole internet. Or to login into your bank accounts and steal directly from your bank. The possibilities are endless here when you think of the power of social engineering and quite harmful.

Impact of social engineering

The impact of social engineering is quite enormous today if you ask. Imagine a company that hates your company and wants to ruin its business; they can easily do this using social engineering. Larger companies spread across several locations are often more vulnerable given their complexity, but smaller companies can also be attacked. From receptionists to security guards to executives to IT personnel, everyone is a potential social engineer victim. Help-desk and call-center employees are especially vulnerable because they are to be helpful and forthcoming with information.

Vast chunks of information can fall into the wrong hands because of this advancement, such as,

- User passwords.

- Security badges or keys to the building and even to the computer room.

- Intellectual property such as design specifications, source code, and other research-and-development documentation.

- Confidential financial reports.

- Private and personal employee information.

- Personally, identifiable information (PII) such as health records and credit card information.

- Customer lists and sales prospects.

A lot more when you come to think of it because if any of this information is leaked or sold to a third party, financial losses, lowered employee morale, decreased customer loyalty, and even legal and regulatory compliance issues could result.

Common targets of SE (Social Engineering)

Upon research, it was found that the people who trust their social network provider were the most vital targets of social engineering. Social engineering is one of the most common types of threats that may face social network users. Training and increasing users' awareness of such dangers is essential for maintaining continuous and safe social networking services. Identifying the most vulnerable users to target them for these training programs is desirable for increasing their effectiveness. Few studies have investigated the effect of individuals' characteristics on predicting their vulnerability to social engineering in the context of social networks. The present study developed a novel model to predict user vulnerability based on user characteristics' several perspectives to address this gap.

SE (Social Engineering) to gather information

With social engineering and people easily trusting different social networks, it is much easier to gather information within few minutes since most information is only a few clicks away if looked into.

The present study investigated user characteristics in social networks, particularly Facebook, from different angles, such as peoples› behavior, perceptions, and socio-emotions, to identify the factors that could predict individuals' vulnerability to SE threats. People's vulnerability levels will be determined based on their response to a variety of social engineering scenarios.

Social networking

Social networking is the most common and effective way to socialize with people online, advertises your business, buy and sell, and is even used for online dating. At this point, everyone has a social media account, be it a kid, teenager, or adult. I don't think we can go on with life without the use of social networking platforms. Depending on the social media platform, members may be able to contact any other member. In other cases, members can contact anyone they have a connection to, and subsequently anyone that contact has a link to, and so on. Some services require members to have a pre-existing relationship to contact other members.

Common Threats

Social networking is an important platform, and it's impossible to be without considering how it has transformed over lives entirely and has had us hooked. It has a very dark side to it too. A few of which we are going to discuss here.

First off in our list comes identity theft. Anyone can act like you by simply taking a few pictures from social media and make an account using your name. This can go wrong since this person can do whatever with your name and image, and you will be the person getting in trouble for it. Next up is how a hacker can hack into your online conversations or sharp pictures and leak them online or use them to blackmail you, or they could sell them to a third party. Other things also involve acting as a legitimate webpage, asking you for your credit card details for your online purchase; this can end miserably as this fake webpage can access your bank accounts and rob you of your money.

You can also fall victim to cyberbullying or catfishing. The catfishing culture revolves around online dating and acting like someone you are not. This is a widespread practice these days.

Your data can also be shared with a third party. Ever wondered how you were talking about a product online with your friends, and all of a sudden, you start seeing ads for this product? That is what most social networks do; they take advantage of your data and try to push ads through your media to lure you into buying things.

Defining and Explaining Malware

What is Malware, we ask? Well, Malware is this software used to cause damage and disruption to computers and computing systems. Malware most often refers to "malicious software." The components and types of this malicious software include spyware, malware, Trojan viruses, ransomware, amongst others discussed below.

- **Viruses**

These form a subgroup of the said malware. It is most often the software that is malicious and baleful and is found attached to certain files. The files and documents connected to support macros to ensure its execution and spread like fire from one host to another. After it is downloaded into the system, it lays dormant. However, as soon as the file is active and open, they begin to work their troubles. They can interrupt the smooth functioning of a system, which often results in concerns with operation and loss of data.

- **Worms**

These can replicate and reproduce to find their way into any device falling within the communication portals. These are different from viruses as they depend on host programs to find their way into spreading. It does the damage by infecting a device through a downloaded document or file or even a network connection before it begins replicating itself and dispersing. The implications of the infection include disruption in operation and the risk of data loss.

- **Trojan viruses**

These are created for a better purpose as per se. Often also termed as 'helpful software' by many. However, once download, the virus holds the ability to find its way through sensitive information and datum. It doesn't just have access to them but can also make changes to it and even delete or block it. This can be detrimental to the function of the device.

- **Spyware**

As the name suggests, this software runs in secret operation on the devices, particularly a computer, and reports the activity back to certain remote users. Unlike the previous malware mentioned, it doesn't interrupt the operations of a device but looks to target important and sensitive data and gives access to the attackers. It is most often used to attain personal information and particularly, financial information. An example can be of keylogger, which functions as a recorder of your keystrokes to save and then leak important data like passwords.

- **Adware**

When talking about Adware, it can be fairly said that it collects data on device usage and tends to provide relevant advertisements to the ones using it. It doesn't necessarily have to be harmful to the device itself, but it can raise issues for the system being used. For example, it can direct your browser to phishing websites and sites that could lead to further malware like Trojan horses. They can also slow the operations of the system.

- **Ransomware**

It is a dangerous software that poses a threat to the sensitive information on a system. It does so by encrypting data to make it unusable by the user. More so, it tends to ask for financial compensation for the information to be released. It is also considered a parcel of the phishing scam at large and makes its way through disguised links as the attacker begins encrypting certain data and adds a lock to it that can only be opened by a mathematical key that only the attacker has access to. As the financial compensation is released, the key is handed over, and data gets unlocked.

Other and non-specific malware includes file-less malware. It operates from the memory of the user's computer and not from any downloaded file or document. The fact that it isn't attached to a particular file is complicated to detect. Difficult detection, of course, leads to a difficult solution to the problem.

Shoulder surfing

Shoulder surfing is an illegal practice that involves the theft of your data by spying over your shoulder when you are using any of your devices in a public setting. It can be theft of your bank details or identity theft; either way, you always need to be mindful of exposing your sensitive information in a public setting. You can never know who is spying on you, which will lead you to some serious trouble.

Eavesdropping

An eavesdropping attack, also known as a sniffing or snooping attack, is a theft of information transmitted over a network by a computer, smartphone, or another connected device.

Eavesdropping is a deceptively mild term. The attackers are usually after sensitive financial and business information that can be sold for criminal purposes. There is also a booming trade in so-called spouse ware, allowing people to eavesdrop on their loved ones by tracking their smartphone use.

Eavesdropping attacks are more straightforward and can be passive, meaning that a piece of software can merely sit along the network lane, collecting all related network traffic for later review. The intruder would not need to be connected to the program continuously. An intruder can use direct injection or a virus or other Malware to install the software on a compromised computer, then return later to recover any data discovered or cause the software to send the data at a specified time. Modification attacks, including eavesdropping attacks, require getting to the right place in the network, but they also need timing. Hackers are actively devising new ways to listen in on online conversations. Protocol analyzers are used to capture voice-over-IP calls that are made using IP-based communication. The data can be transformed into audio files, which the hacker can then interpret. Data sniffing is another common eavesdropping technique. On local networks that use a HUB, this approach works well. Since all network messages are delivered to all network ports, all a sniffer has to do is opt to accept any piece of incoming data, even though it was not meant for the intended recipients. If unsecured information is broadcast to all network ports, wireless networking data may be equally abused. There are ways you can prevent this from happening. Above that, Cybersecurity researchers are now working around the clock to ensure that web communications are as safe as possible. Possible ways to overcome this are as follows:

One of the most critical responsibilities of cybersecurity professionals is to create digital networks for their businesses that can survive hacker attacks and are resistant to digital eavesdropping attempts. Protection professionals use several firewalls and antivirus tools to guarantee that any data passing between the network's nodal points are not accessible to hackers who may have reached a specific port. Another way being; Encrypting data as it is transferred across digital networks is a significant part of what a cyber-security specialist does. Encryption is the process of scrambling data before delivering it to the recipient so that anyone attempting to decipher it sees a string of gibberish. On the other hand, the recipient has an encryption key that can safely and securely decrypt the message and retrieve the content. Much too many internet users have no idea how to keep their data safe or trust in old security methods that have long ago been rendered useless by modern and advanced hacking techniques. Working as a cyber-security specialist with an organization involves explaining cybersecurity fundamentals to those who access the company's computer network daily. You'll need to show them how to use a good password, update it regularly, and stop uploading or opening unfamiliar files from the internet, and other security fundamentals that will help secure the company's network.

Dumpster Diving

Dumpster diving is a method used in information technology to recover information used to attack a computer network. Dumpster diving isn't all about looking through garbage for obvious gems like sticky notes or access codes or passwords printed on them. Information that seems to be innocuous, such as a contact list, schedule, or organizational map, may be used to help an intruder obtain entry to a network using social engineering techniques. Latest studies have shown that identity fraud and other associated offenses have become increasingly common. It turned out this way because hackers knew how to collect relevant information such as credit card invoices, statements of accounts, and other classified information just by digging at one's garbage. These pieces of data are then paired with the data that a person posts on social networking sites. There are some reported cases of this practice taking place in the computer world. In the most well-known case of Larry Ellison, Oracle's CEO engaged private investigators to search the Microsoft dumpsters for valuable details. That was an attempt to collect information about future activities to sustain the case.

Furthermore, in 2001, the shampoo competition between rivals Proctor & Gamble and Unilever was described as a target of industrial espionage. Proctor and Gamble prosecutors rummaged through recycling bins outside the Unilever Corporations. They were influential in obtaining critical information about industry research, forecasts, and upcoming goods. The two companies, on the other side, came up with an out-of-the-box approach. The two companies, on the other hand, reached an out-of-court settlement. Your 'trash' can be saved if specific cautions could be implemented while you go about your work.

A variety of service organizations provides monitoring surveillance programs. The remote monitoring camera assists their programs. They should automatically report any anomalies near the dumpsters to the security authority if they find them. CDs or DVDs containing personal data, such as images, videos, or other classified material, should be destroyed. When servers, printers, cell phones, or other hardware no longer serve a need, they must be washed and all data erased to avoid any problems. Experts recommend that the organization develop a recycling program in which all material, including printouts, is shredded in a cross-cut shredder before being recycled, all storage media is erased, and all workers are informed about the risks of untracked waste to discourage dumpster divers from discovering valuable something from the garbage.

Phishing

The question is, what do we understand by phishing? Phishing is a sort of attack that involves sending fraudulent communications that appear to come from a reputable source. It is usually performed through email. The goal is to steal sensitive data like credit card and login information or install malware on the victim's machine. Phishing is a common type of cyber-attack that everyone should learn about to protect themselves.

Countermeasures for Social Networking

While you are social networking, you need to be mindful of many things starting from having a solid password for not giving your information on faulty or shady social networks. We have more tips for you.

The first thing in this regard would be to avoid clicking on any attachments or links that come your way. It is the favorite ploy from cybercriminals as many people often find themselves tricked into clicking these links that could come from anywhere, even their banks. Read thoroughly before you click. Another thing would be to use unique passwords, which are complex and cannot easily be broken into. Make use of special characters like symbols to ensure better safety.

Thirdly, make sure to keep your identity safe. Understand that passwords need not be shared and also should be changed often. Make use of the likes of two-factor authentication if available.

Back-up your data: If ransomware, Malware infects your computer, or it crashes, the only way to ensure that you will be able to retrieve your lost data is by backing it up and doing so regularly. This also means that if you mislay data or accidentally delete something, it can always be recovered.

Ensure that you have a robust and up-to-date internet security package running – With online threats becoming increasingly more sophisticated and cybercriminals willing to jump on any social trend to spread Malware, the online threat landscape is changing drastically by the minute. Security software from a recognized name like Norton is the best and safest option for stopping malicious software from installing on your PC as it can prevent it from taking over or slowing down your system.

Keep all software on your PC up-to-date with the latest updates and patches. By keeping your software up-to-date, potential vulnerabilities (including zero-day) can be patched and help keep cybercriminals and hackers at bay.

Installing modern web browser

Modern browsers tend to render successfully sits that you built using all the necessary standards and directions. One doesn't require any specific hacks to attain complete performance as they find their way through it.

These browsers are fast as they ensure to take complete advantage of the platform and renders graphics with the help of the GPU. It compiles and then also executes Javascript across multiple CPU cores and ensures that these applications are on the same speed as their native applications.

Other benefits include better and more inclusive experiences like native applications and also video content, vectors, and texts without hampering performance.

Heeding unsafe site warnings

Often, we come across sites where we get a warning from our web browser that we are trying to gain access to might not be safe.

Google will sometimes include a textual warning on risky search results, too. These notices should be heeded. Stay away from potentially compromised sites to keep your data safe. Upon accessing these websites, we might be at a loss since they can take advantage of our sensitive information and maybe sell it elsewhere, so one needs to take these warnings seriously and not just ignore them.

Integrating with antivirus software

Antivirus software, also known as anti-malware software (abbreviated to AV software), is a computer application that stops, detects, and eliminates Malware. Antivirus software was designed to identify and kill computer viruses, as the name implies. However, as other ransomware types became more prevalent, antivirus applications began to offer protection against different device threats. Frederick B. Cohen's 1987 demonstration that no algorithm can perfectly identify all potential viruses is one of the few solid scientific findings in computer virus analysis. However, by utilizing several layers of protection, a high detection rate can be attained. As malware attacks grow in number and scope, more advanced anti-malware technologies are needed to protect files, processes, and records. The financial opportunity for attackers, especially for companies, is not going anywhere. Traditional anti-malware technologies are unlikely to be successful enough as ransomware-as-a-service, targeted phishing, IoT hacking, and even malicious nation-state actors broaden and change the threat environment. Antivirus APIs allow fast scanning to guard against malicious file uploads, web traffic, and other attacks. An antivirus program built directly into the system is much easier, minimizing scan times to milliseconds. Since a single anti-malware engine is prone to ignore attacks, it's safer to use several machines if at all necessary. Often websites and web apps need visitors to upload files, which are then saved on the web servers of the site or service. While this is a valuable and, in some situations, necessary feature, it often presents a significant security risk if adequate protections are not enforced. Malicious code can be imported by attackers and executed when the files are accessed. The easiest solution is to integrate with anti-malware scanning tools to check all file uploads for Malware, and malicious files are identified. This form of anti-malware integration generally requires the use of anti-malware APIs.

Using automatic updates

When flaws with software systems are detected, the developer patches them. Users may use automatic upgrades to keep their device applications up to date without searching for and installing updates manually. The app scans for available updates automatically, and if any are detected, they are downloaded and updated without user interaction. The most prominent example you can find is your OS that runs your device's entirety, be it a laptop, console, phone, or tablet. Auto upgrades for the Microsoft Windows operating system help keep Windows up to date with the new bug patches, feature improvements, and other improvements. Automatic upgrades aid in the protection of apps from malware and hacking attempts. Of course, your update strategy should be customized to your specific requirements. However, for the following, a well-designed update strategy would depend on automated updates:

Security flaws are critical. Since the consequences of these vulnerability flaws are so high, fixing proven, zero-day security bugs immediately are worth the cost and potential inconvenience of workloads—updates to the operating system. Vendors typically extensively test patches for the operating system. Software upgrades may or may not be thoroughly vetted before being sent out and are less dangerous to submit—updates with applications that can be rolled back with ease. The power to "roll back" a device, or return it to a previous state of time, is good protection against failed upgrades. Rollbacks are also simple to do on virtualized or containerized environments since virtual discs or container images may be restored to earlier states. Few operating systems have built-in rollback capabilities, but these are less reliable. Windows

An automatic Update is an outstanding tool for notifying you about security updates. It's also an excellent way to get updates if you only have a few devices to support and don't think bandwidth usage would be a problem. Windows Automatic Update is an outstanding tool for notifying you about security updates. It's also an excellent way to get updates if you only have a few devices to support and don't think bandwidth usage would be a problem. There may also be occasions when it is preferable to use the option to deploy updates on a fixed timeline, but be vigilant since a closer analysis of the issue shows a drawback to automatic updates.

Private browsing

You may be concerned about protecting your online privacy as cyber-attacks, and emerging threats continue to develop. And it's not without excuse. Cybercriminals can get their hands on your details to steal your identities and commit other crimes. What would you do to protect your privacy when browsing the internet or doing business online? Using a private tab is an intelligent thing. First, bear in mind that regular web surfing on a public Wi-Fi network exposes your web searches, purchases, and other personal data to third parties. Online service companies, government departments, colleges, directories, marketers, other consumers of the computers, and others using the same unsecured Wi-Fi network are all potential perpetrators. In the most abstract form, privacy refers to the state of not being watched or interrupted by someone. Data protection refers to the ability to monitor how your data is stored and processed in the digital world. Since your sensitive information helps identity thieves and other cybercriminals that can sell it on the dark web, your privacy is essential. Web browsers with private browsing functionality can assist with this. When you allow private browsing, you can keep your Internet sessions secret from other users on the same machine or smartphone. Your temporary browsing data — browsing history, search information, and cookies — will not be saved by the web browser if you use private browsing modes. Some private surfing modes are capable of erasing stored or bookmarked files. Some also have anti-tracking functionality that can help you conceal your location. The best example and the most famous one for this are the incognito modes on Google chrome. It is the most widely used medium of private browsing where you are met with a very user-friendly setup, just like the standard chrome, and gives way to smooth surfing.

Protective measures

When it comes to information security, most people don't care about it until there's a crisis, and by then, a breakdown of protection will create severe problems. We have answers to some commonly asked questions about possible security vulnerabilities and how you can discourage them from happening to you because we all want to keep our machines and information secure. With the ongoing digitization of virtually every domain in the last few years and the increase in web network usage with the current pandemic, a considerable amount of personal data has been more exposed on the internet. As a result, the computer is vulnerable to security breaches and the leaking of sensitive information. Many large-scale data and security violations have happened in history, including the 2013 hack of 1 billion Yahoo users. As a result of the present situation, cyber and information security has become one of the most critical issues of the new digitalized world. If our computers and other systems are not adequately secured, certain risks emerge. Connecting and then securing your computer means identifying and stopping unauthorized access to your computer by hackers. As countermeasures, a list of software could be availed to aid you in protecting your computer or other devices from peril. The following are some examples of software that is important to your computer's security:

Antivirus software is the most common method of protection used by any type of device. It protects you from viruses that can tamper with your data and slow down your computer's performance. As new viruses emerge regularly, this program must be revised periodically.

Good firewall software allows you to navigate the internet and search through many channels safely. The firewall prevents unauthorized users from accessing your device by blocking unauthorized traffic.

Anti-Spyware Software: Spywares are applications that can be mounted on your computer to leak your data to a third-party website. Passwords, credit card numbers, and Social Security numbers are examples of valuable records. This software, too, must be revised daily to provide the best protection against data loss.

Other than software aiding you in protecting your device, you too can contribute to safety by taking care of how and what you use on your device. A small yet excellent example being, downloading information and data from verified publishers. Applications for your laptop and phone help you perform tasks, but some of these apps can be bogus. Be sure to download them from authors that have been verified by the store of the device you are using.

Another little thing would be not to share any of your credentials with anyone. Especially if you are working in a business environment as your entire establishment could be in jeopardy.

Identity theft

Most frequently committed cybercrime was Social network fraud, Identity theft, spreading hate and Inciting terrorism, Cyberbullying, online Impersonation, Cyber extortion, Child pornography, and Unauthorized system access; as we move on to the 2020's some of the leading cyber threats include Social engineering attacks, Phishing, Ransomware, IoT-Based attacks, Deepfake, AI-Enhanced cyberthreats, AI Fuzzing, Machine Learning Poisoning, Smart contract hacking, cloud vulnerability, etc.

Chapter 7
Cyber Attacks and Survival

Knowledge, However, is Power

Identity theft has been around for centuries and is a serious issue that can affect many life areas. It could prohibit anyone from getting a credit card or receiving approval for a housing loan or car loan, and most importantly, it could ruin chances of getting a job. The rise of technology in the late 20th century ushered in a new identity fraud era; crime is more common and devastating.

Modern life has afforded us unprecedented conveniences. But it also opens the door to deceptive criminality schemes. Fraudsters can attack online or offline, hiding behind the facade of phony emails, text messages, and telephone calls. According to the financial consulting firm Javelin Strategy & Research, 13 million consumers fell victim in 2019, costing them $3.5 billion in out-of-pocket costs. The recent study, Javelin's 2021 identity fraud study, provides a comprehensive analysis of fraud trends in the context of a changing technological and payment landscape to inform consumers, financial institutions, and businesses about the most effective means for controlling identity fraud. The report talks about the shift from traditional identity fraud to unconventional, bizarre identity frauds. The transformed identity fraud during the COVID-19 pandemic rose to a total of $56 billion in 2020, resulting in $43 billion in losses to

U.S. consumers alone. Consumers are more vulnerable and are directly targeted by fraudsters; this allows the fraudsters to bypass the complex and secured fraud-detection barriers maintained by financial service providers. Consumers remain a target as the stimulus bill is passed into law, unemployment benefit scams, and economic impact payment check fraud should be a priority for all financial services. Mitigating future stimulus bills related to cyber fraud risks, building and maintaining consumer trust has been one of the challenges for financial institutions.

There are different forms of Identity theft; let's discuss few important ones in detail:

1. Account takeover fraud

2. Mail ID Theft

3. Debit/Credit Card Fraud

4. Driver's License ID Theft

5. Medical ID theft

6. Biometric ID Theft

7. Online Shopping Fraud

8. Social Security Number ID Theft

9 Home Title and Mortgage Fraud

10. Tax ID Theft

11. Child ID Theft

12. Passport ID Theft

13. Senior ID Theft and scams

14. Internet of Things (IoT) I.D. Theft.

Account takeover fraud is when someone gains access and takes control of accounts without your knowledge or permission. This account can be used to make fraudulent transactions, money transfers, etc.

Account takeover fraud accounted for 53% of all existing account fraud in 2019, according to Javelin. According to Kaspersky fraud prevention research statistics, Account takeover fraud increased from 34% in 2019 to 54% in 2020. There has been a spike in social engineering techniques and fraudulent schemes by cybercriminals. There are two ways the scam takes place; the first tactic sees scammer masquerade as "the rescuer" where they pretend to be security experts trying to save you from suspicious charges or payment fraud and offer help. They may extract personal information and ask the victim to install an app for remote management, pretending to troubleshoot. The second tactic could be cybercriminals acting as "the investor" from investment companies or investment banks for investments in shares or cryptocurrencies. Legitimate remote access tools (RAT) like TeamViewer were used in an attempt to gain access to user accounts. A fraudster posing from a legitimate financial institution trying to help you by being your rescuer may ask you to download the Any Desk or TeamViewer app software to access or control your computer and bank accounts. Once access is gained, the fraudsters will transfer money out of the victim's account. The Reserve Bank of India (RBI) warned people about the Any Desk app used by the fraudsters to steal people's money via Unified Payment Interface (UPI).

Some of the measures that can be followed to avoid such attacks are

1. Limit the number of attempts to conduct a transaction.

2. Be aware of such possible tricks fraudsters could use.

3. Make sure your financial institutions are conducting annual security audits and penetration tests.

4. Ensure your financial institution has a fraud analysis team capable of finding and analyzing the emerging methods fraudsters are using.

5. Use multi-factor authentication to minimize the chance of accounts being taken over.

6. Finally, if required, install a fraud prevention solution that can quickly identify the fraud.

Mail Identity Theft: This is the most sophisticated type of Identity Theft in recent years. This scam may involve stealing checks from mailboxes, altering them, and encashing them. Another scam is that the con artist has been known to intercept credit and debit cards to rack up unauthorized charges. Watch out for the mails you throw; anything containing account statements, banking information, or other personal details can be stolen and used against you. Mail theft or tampering can be reported to your local postal inspection services. Debit/Credit Card Fraud: When someone uses your card without your knowledge, the fraud occurs; criminals may also make unauthorized, fraudulent transactions without having a physical card in hand. Card number, PIN, CVV number, and other related information on the card need to be always protected. This fraudulent activity could affect the credit in several ways, causing credit card balance to spike or hurting your credit scores.

If you suspect any fraudulent transaction or credit/debit card misuse, contact your card provider immediately, as most of them have systems in place to prevent and identify credit card fraud. The dollar amount of attempted fraudulent transactions rose 35% in April 2020, according to Fidelity National Information Inc - a banking fraud detection company.

1. Before entering your credit card account information on the website, make sure it starts with "HTTPS" and has a grey padlock symbol to make sure that the website is secure.

2. Avoid shopping from public WIFI hotspots, as anyone on the network can grab the information.

3. Make sure you use your credit card on a trusted and secured website and do not save the card information on any website without multi-factor authentication. Your credit card details are cheap; crooks can steal information and sell it on the Dark Web. Dark Web is a hard-to-find website and forum for fraudsters; it's a marketplace for many types of illegal activities.

According to Experian, credit/debit card details are sold on the dark web for a mere $5 with the CVV number and up to $110 if it has a higher financial limit, with all information like Social Security Number, Date of Birth, complete account number, and other personal data. It's safe to enroll in an identity theft monitoring service; these services continuously scan the wide expanse of the dark web for information about you that may be for sale. If the company finds information on the deal, they will immediately send an alert. It is important to inform the credit card company to replace the credit card with a new number.

A United States sentencing report found that 75% of credit card offenders are males in their mid-30's. The report also found that 38% were black, 31% were Hispanics, 25% were Whites, and around 5% to 6% were other races. Protect your credit card and personal information by reducing paper trials; have all your credit card and banking correspondence sent to you electronically. Driver's License ID Theft: Driver's license contains your name and address and your birth date and identifying characteristics like height, weight, and a photo. The magnetic strip or barcode on the back of the driver's license card gives anyone who swipes your license through a scanner even more information.

Equifax executives revealed the true scope of a breach. In their statement to the Securities and Exchange Commission, the company said 17.6 million consumers had their driver's license number exposed, and another 38,000 people had their full driver's license compromised. Cybercriminals sell driver's rights on the Dark Web for about $20 a piece. Once a driver's license is compromised, a criminal could falsely use it during a traffic stop to avoid a citation-which means it could end up on your driving record. It could also lead to an erroneous warrant for arrest, so it's important to report the DMV and the local police authorities' theft. Medical ID theft: Medical identity theft is growing exponentially; criminals may use your name or health insurance number to get care for themselves.

According to the Identity Theft Research center, the medical care sector had the second-highest data breaches in 2019. It results in bills for medical services, prescriptions, and medical products you never requested or received. Make it a habit to review your medical statements and claims regularly to spot fraud and take steps to remedy it. You can file a health privacy complaint with the U.S. Department of Health and Human Services online or by calling when you suspect Medicare fraud. Biometric ID Theft, this type of theft involves stealing or spoofing a person's physical or behavioral characteristics to unlock a device, like facial or voice recognition to unlock a phone or tap into the machine.

This gives them access to private information and digital wallets. Store the biometric information safely and update all the devices as recommended. Online Shopping Fraud: Online shopping on unfamiliar WIFI networks, such as coffee shops or any common commercial centers. Criminals may hack their way into the websites and use your saved cards to make unapproved purchases. It's always smart to shop, bank, or handle sensitive information on a trusted private WIFI network. Also, watch out for secure and safe websites, pay attention to the URL of the website. If you're skeptical, don't access the website to purchase or shop anything online— Social Security Number (SSN) I.D. Theft: SSN can be a powerful tool for a fraudster to get their hands on other personal information that can be used to open fraudulent accounts.

This can lead to delinquent accounts showing up on credit reports and affecting credit scores. Keeping SSNs in a safe place and checking credit reports regularly is very important. Those who have been victimized can report it to the Social Security Administration and notify their state's tax office. Home Title and Mortgage Fraud, the components of your identity can be stolen by criminals when they have access to the home title or property papers. They may be able to transfer the ownership to themselves. They can use your home equity to gain access to loans and lines of credit.

Repercussions could be quite shocking if the rightful owner faces unexpected foreclosure notices. Prevent home title fraud by periodically checking your home information with your county's deed office. Watch out for your regular mortgage bills, tax bills, and other bills. If you suddenly stop receiving these bills, that's another potential cause of alarm. Mortgage account numbers could reveal a lot of personal information about the buyer or seller. This information could help the criminal take a home equity line of credit or second mortgage. In such cases, the Mortgage lender should be informed. Tax ID Theft: Beware of anyone posing as IRS officials requesting your personal information on phone calls or emails.

The IRS will never contact a person by phone or email without first sending notice through the mail. If you are a victim of tax identity theft, fill out an identity theft Affidavit with the IRS or respective state tax department. Roughly 34% of identity theft and fraud complaints are exclusive to tax and employment fraud. Child ID Theft: According to a 2019 Javelin Strategy and Research report, more than 1 million children in the U.S. were victims of identity theft, and two-third were younger than eight years old. A relative or a family member committed 18% of identity fraud cases against minors. Families paid $540 million in out-of-pocket expenses to rectify the issues. These IDs can be used for many reasons like open accounts, obtain credit cards, etc. File a police complaint if you suspect that your child's identity is stolen. Passport ID Theft: A valid travel document can fetch a hefty price on the Dark Web, causing trouble to the victims who have lost the passport.

Suppose your passport number is compromised U.S. department or any country recommends reporting it as lost or stolen. In that case, this will subsequently invalidate the passport, and it can no longer be used for international travel. Senior ID Theft and scams: Elderly citizens are particularly vulnerable to cybercriminals; tech scammers could call and get sensitive information like passwords and card numbers. Criminals represent themselves from the IRS office or Medicare office to gain trust; sometimes, senior citizens are deceived when they are called by cybercriminals posing as grandchildren who are in trouble and need money. 1 in 4 victims of identity theft is aged 60 and older, according to the U.S. Insurance Information Institute. The odds of being a victim of fraud are high with an increase in age; baby boomers (people born between 1946 and 1964, approximately 71 million in the U.S.) constitute 42.6% who have been victims of credit card fraud, which is the highest.

It's always safe to check credit card reports regularly, daily, or weekly and opt for a text or email alerts every time a transaction is made. If there are any suspicious transactions, inform the card agencies and dispute the charges. Internet of Things (IoT) I.D. Theft, Everything from household appliances to smartphones to cars is now synced up to the internet and linked to one and other. When someone exploits a security flaw in an internet-connected device to access your data, there is a chance of IoT exploitation. Since there are many devices connected, every device becomes an entry point for a hacker.

If you find anything fishy, change the passwords on all the interconnected devices — secure the home's wireless network with a secure password. Over 1.6+ billion records were compromised between January 1, 2005, to August 31, 2019. People worry more about Identity theft than murder; the primary reason for the concern is the high number of data breaches, and prevalence of hacking, and the feeling of vulnerability. According to Atlas VPN research paper, credit card fraud occurrences rose 161% in 2020. Emotional Impacts of being a fraud victim are intense; according to the Identity Theft Resource Center Report, 54% of people reported a sense of helplessness or powerlessness, 69% expressed fear over their financial safety, 42% felt fear for the financial security of their family members.

Different types of thefts are on the rise, every day, there is an innovative way of stealing information, and the numbers are striking. But knowledge, however, is power. Knowing what action to take at the right time is the most important skill of the era.

Chapter 8
Future Crimes:

Safety should be the new Lifestyle

Smartphones are turning human beings into human sensors, generating tons of information about us. As a result, we are living our lives in the shadow of massive digital footprints. Data is constantly being generated around us; the data creation cycle never sleeps. A lot is happening every minute online; people are checking emails, sending text messages, shopping, watching videos, posting pictures, and much more. Global online content consumption nearly doubled in 2020, compared to 2019. A new study of over 10,000 people in five countries says that an average daily spent consuming content is now six hours and 59 minutes, including phone, T.V., and other forms of digital media. Global lockdown due to Coronavirus has been attributed to this surge. Connected T.V. (CTV) and Over the Top (OTT) are the biggest beneficiaries, with > 44% of all consumers using CTV devices accessing Netflix, Prime Video, Hulu, Hotstar, Peacock, and Disney+, etc., YouTube, and Tok-Tok have seen increased Interest and the highest growth, with YouTube having 43% of consumers spending time on the YouTube platform. Tok-Tok active users in the U.S. grew from 52.1 million in August 2020 to 53.5 million; in early September 2020, the Tok-Tok app had an additional 150,000 to 200,000 new installs daily throughout September.

Every minute of the day, 26k Apps are downloaded, 3.47MM videos watched on YouTube, 510K comments posted on Facebook, 694k videos viewed on Tok-Tok, 350k tweets sent on Twitter, 97.2k hours of content consumed on Netflix, 21MM Snaps created on Snapchat, 7K active users in LinkedIn, 4.2MM Google Searches on Google, $283K spent on Amazon online shopping, 12.55K Ride-share taken on Uber and Lyft, and the 2021 Internet minutes statistics list goes on. According to Gartner, a leading research and advisory company, the worldwide information security market is forecast to reach $170.4 billion in 2022.

With these recent trends and increasing usage of the internet, cybersecurity issues are a matter of concern for every netizen. The rollout of 5G has made connected devices more connected than ever. 2020 has brought about many turmoil and changes; COVID-19 has forced companies to create remote workforces and operate off cloud-based platforms. Cybercrimes could be on the rise, and the cybersecurity industry has never been more important. Two thousand twenty-one cybersecurity statistics and figures show that remote workers will be the target for cybercriminals. Cloud breaches will increase, and the Internet of Things (IoT) will become more vulnerable to cyber-attacks, and the cybersecurity skills gap will remain an issue.

This new digital transformation journey which includes remote work, Internet of Things (IoT), bring-your-own-device (BYOD), and cloud initiatives, gives hackers new ways to infiltrate any organization exponentially the attack surface. The sudden surge in technologies like Artificial Intelligence (A.I.) and Machine Learning (ML) gives hackers new and innovative tools to vector in on high-end targets, reach bigger and more diverse audiences by distributing malicious software. According to Splunk, a company headquartered in California, which captures, indexes, and correlates real-time data, there are 50 top Cybersecurity threats that we need to watch out for in 2021. The report lists out all the 50 top security threats that the cybercriminals are aiming at, as the technologies are evolving rapidly and know malware samples having surpassed the one billion mark making it very difficult for any Netizen to keep the cybercriminals at bay.

Some of the security threats listed are Account Takeover, Bill Fraud, Business Invoice Fraud, Compromised Credentials, Cloud crypto mining, Command and Control, DDoS attack, DNS Hijacking, Host redirection, IoT threats, Network sniffing, Shadow I.T., Social Engineering Attacks, Disabling Security Tools, Macro Viruses, Insider Threats, Pass the Hash, Phishing, Whale Phishing, Spear Phishing, Ransomware, SIM jacking, Spyware, Typosquatting, Wire attack, XSS, Zero Day Exploitation, etc. According to Booz Allen Hamilton, an American consulting firm with expertise in analytics, digital, engineering, and Cyber, lists eight key cyber threat trends to watch out for in 2021.

The report talks about how the Malware business model is evolving for NextGen extortion; Ransomware attack is one thing that has increased during COVID and is here to stay. According to Monster Cloud, the FBI sees a significant spike in ransomware attacks during the pandemic, expanding the attack by 300%-400%. Monster Cloud, a leading expert in cyberterrorism and ransomware recovery, has analyzed the stats, surveys, and studies to find the ransomware trends that will loom large in 2021. Ransomware as a Service (RaaS) is much easier for hackers. There are now ransomware gangs and readily available ransomware software for sale, which gives relatively cheap and easy access to malicious programs. RaaS providers take a 20% - 30% cut of the ransom profit generated. Some of the ransomware gangs who provide ransomware attacks as service are Net walker/Mail to, DopplePaymer, Ryuk, Ravi/Sodinokibi, Egregor, etc.; most of these gangs have originated from Russia and Europe.

Healthcare-related attacks around the world have doubled in the year 2020; some of the countries affected due to ransomware are Srilanka, Russia, Mexico, France, Turkey, India, China, U.S., etc. Many companies are working on putting an I.T. plan in place to stop threats before they happen, but this does not dissuade the Cybercriminals. They are using this as an opportunity to move to a different medium, mobile attacks. There has been more than a 30% increase in Mobile ransomware in 2020. Ransomware gangs use Adware, Trojans, Risk Tools, Backdoor, and Exploit to attack mobile devices. Once the mobile is infected, they could steal sensitive data from smartphones or lock the device, and they may trick the victim into downloading mobile ransomware through social networking schemes.

After the malware is downloaded onto the device, it shows a fake message accusing the victim of unlawful engagement before encrypting files and locking the device. They may demand payment, often via Bitcoin, to return the data or unlock the device; once the payment is processed, they will send a code to decrypt the data and unlock the phone. Crypto locker infected more than 10,000 computers; the hackers wanted $300 from each victim in exchange for a decryption code. It's essential to protect mobile devices from ransomware:

1. Use common sense and stay informed about the latest threats.

2. Be Cautious and wary of installing fake apps

3. Install security patches regularly.

4. Make sure you back up all important files.

5. Delete unwanted apps.

6. Use a robust mobile security solution as a last resort.

Ransomware attacks are always opportunistic. The attacker's motive is mostly profit. So, prevention is always better; some of the tactics or techniques that these attackers use at various phases to gain access and control over your device or system before they launch cyber-attacks are well documented by The MITRE Corporation, an American not-for-profit organization. The MITRE ATT&CK framework has been around for years that describe tactics, techniques, and procedures used by the attackers. The ATT&CK categories are as below:

1. Initial Access

2. Execution

3. Persistence

4. Privilege Escalation

5. Defense Evasion

6. Credential Access

7. Discovery

8. Lateral Movement

9. Collection

10. Command and Control (C2)

11. Exfiltration

12. Impact

The first six categories aim to gain access to the target's network and systems; attackers use three methods to access the target initially.

- Social Engineering or Phishing method to install malware without the users' awareness.

- They may use legitimate credentials exposed via data breach to get access.

- They may exploit a vulnerability in an internet application or service. Mobile devices are small, and the user interface makes it very difficult for users to evaluate email or web page legitimacy.

People use it while walking, driving, talking, and doing many activities, limiting their ability to pay close attention to details. This is one main reason why a lot of mobile users are susceptible to attacks. Experts predict that there will be a ransomware attack every 11 seconds in 2021, and according to industry predictions, there will be almost six ransomware attacks every minute in 2021. Ransomware perpetrators carry out more than 4000 attacks every day, and 1 in 3000 emails contains malware. According to an article on safe at last.co blog, which publishes the latest statistics and reports on safety, the global cost associated with ransomware recovery will exceed $20 billion in 2021. The biggest challenge and threat while building castles in the cloud is cloud security.

Cloud refers to servers accessed over the internet and the software and database that run on those servers. These servers are located in data centers spread out all over the world in different countries. Users and companies using cloud computing don't have to own a physical server or run expensive software, databases, or applications on their machines. The cloud enables the users to access the same files and applications from almost any device, as the data is stored on servers in a data center instead of locally on the user's device. Some of the advantages of cloud computing are:

1. Cost-saving, companies can save a lot by reducing their investment in technology. The pay-as-you-use system applies to data storage and computing.

2. Competitive Edge.

3. Security, the cloud host's full-time job, monitors safety more efficiently than a conventional in-house system.

4. Flexibility in using extra bandwidth, cloud-based services can meet demand instantly.

5. Mobility allows mobile access to corporate data via smartphones or any other device.

6. Quality Control, consistent monitoring, and reporting.

7. Disaster Recovery downtime in business is efficiently handled and controlled.

8. Automatic software updates, applications are automatically refreshed and updated, providing continuous security.

9. Sustainability, its more environmentally friendly and results in less carbon footprint.

10. With increased collaboration, team members can view and share information easily and securely across the cloud platform.

Dell reports that companies that invest in big data, cloud, mobility, and security enjoy up to 53% faster revenue growth than their competitors. Given all these advantages, 94% of enterprises are already using cloud services. Public cloud infrastructure is said to grow by 35% in 2021 and will continue to grow for any foreseeable future. Cloud services include Infrastructure as a Service (IaaS), Platform as a Service (PaaS), Software as a Service (SaaS), and Function as a Service (FaaS). The widespread adoption of cloud computing services has left the doors open for attacks by threat actors deploying ransomware or crypto miners.

Threat actors use Saas solutions exfiltrating data from compromised hosts via message to account on widely used webmail. Attacks can include inserting malicious code into applications and widely used software libraries. Threat actors abuse PaaS solutions by redirecting the users of a targeted service to malicious Infrastructure. Some of the biggest cloud security challenges in 2021 that organizations would be worried about are Data Breach. Failure to deal with data properly opens up huge compliance and business risks.

1. Compliance with Regulatory Mandates, small and mid-size companies assume that they are secured with cloud services failing to understand that they need to address additional industry mandates like Payment Card Industry Data Security Standards (PCI DSS), Federal Information Security Modernization Act (FISMA), Gramm-Leach-Bliley

Act (GLBA), Health Insurance Portability and Accountability Act (HIPAA) and Family Educational Rights and Privacy Act (FERPA).

2. Lack of I.T. Expertise in the industry has discouraged more than 34% of the companies from adopting cloud computing. Lack of these skill sets is one of the major threats to the industry.

3. Cloud Migration Issues emerge when the migration process is very complicated and not broken into stages to reduce the risk of critical errors that could corrupt the data.

4. Unsecured Application Programming Interface (APIs) could be an entry point of attack; intruders can hijack data by hacking into less-secure APIs.

5. Insider Threats are when an employee is responsible and involved in malicious activity; more than 43% of all breaches are due to Insider Threats.

6. Open-Source packages are vulnerable; hackers poison Gilt Repo, waiting for developers to use the box and later compromise the application through an attack.

Artificial Intelligence (A.I.) and Machine Learning are used to build malware that can defeat A.I.-based security solutions, and the threat actor goes undetected during or after the attack. There is a rising cyber risk to the parcel and shipping services sector; with the coronavirus pandemic, there is a shift in consumer behavior. Online shopping rose more than 35% from 2019. Consumers are accustomed to receiving multiple order status emails, delivery notifications, package receipts, return labels, etc.; phishing attempts have increased to target the consumers.

Some of the scams that could come up are Ransomware, Reshipping scams, strategic disruption of delivery, and service, which might impact critical services. Mandated contact tracing Apps may open doors for Large-Scale cyber-attacks; exploring and managing Apps' use would be vital in 2021. Cybercriminals likely to capitalize on U.S. telehealth adoption, it is important to watch out for Billing fraud, Ransomware, Phishing, and credential theft; Remote Patient Monitor (RPM) devices must maintain confidentiality, integrity, and availability of patient data and ensure patient safety. 5G to expand the attack surface for Industrial IoT and increase security pressure on mobile hotspots. 5G modems and hotspots are expected to replace existing internet connections, resulting in poor security compromising our data.

Chapter 9
Deep web and Deep Fake

What do you need to watch out for?

Let's imagine the Internet as an Onion, with layers upon layers. The first and outermost layer, which is easy to peel or access, is the internet and is publicly accessible. As we dig deeper into the next layer or second layer hidden beneath is the Deep Web. Deep Web, invisible web, or hidden web makes up the majority of the Internet because it is all the content you can't find and are not indexed on search engines, such as company's internal website pages, private databases, webmail, online banking, restricted social-media profiles, and other sensitive information.

According to The Journal of Electronic Publishing, Deep Web contains 7,500 terabytes of information than 19 terabytes of information on the surface web; it contains 550 billion individual documents compared to one billion of the surface web also contains more than 200,000 deep websites. The total quality content of the deep web is 1000 to 2000 times greater than that of the surface web. The dark web is a conglomeration of different websites with hidden identities and geographic locations; these websites are very difficult to be accessed via standard web browsers or search engines. Tor browser is the home of the dark web and one of the main access points for the dark web as it can hide IP addresses of its users using a bouncing method. When a user accesses the website on Tor, Tor bounces the request for site access to multiple computers worldwide that volunteers maintain.

As the request bounces around computers, the site access request is encrypted and decrypted, which means that the request's source cannot be detected, and nobody can tell where the request came from, making it difficult to track the user and activities. Tor was created with good intentions, but people found an innovative way to use it for sinister purposes where more than 50% of the websites on the dark web are used for criminal purposes. It is an illegal online marketplace for buying and selling illicit goods like - weapons, drugs, stolen credit cards, stolen account passwords, Social Security Numbers, fake identities, etc. The hackers obtain all these stolen goods through hacking into businesses and personal devices.

Bitcoin is a cryptocurrency that is most prevalent and facilitates sales on the dark web. With the release of private browsing networks like Tor in 2002, a collection of shady websites, illegal contents on the websites, and their followers' community began to emerge in full force. The release of Bitcoin in 2009 that facilitated transactions anonymously boosted the sales on the dark web, leaving no paper trails of PayPal or credit cards.

Silk Road was an online modern darknet market, best known for selling illegal drugs. It was a dark web that operated as Tor hidden service. The silk road was launched in 2011, and provided goods and services to over 100,000 buyers, and drew close to a million users at one point. In 2013, the FBI completed a sting and shut down the Silk Road website. The Darknet child pornography website called Playpen was created in August 2014; the website has over 215,000 users and hosted 23,000 erotic, explicit images and videos of children as young as toddlers. Playpen was hosted as a hidden service via Tor browser, which became the reason for the FBI's struggle to track down the servers and locations.

FBI used malware-based network investigative techniques to hack into the users' web browsers accessing the site, thereby revealing their identities. The operation led to the arrest of 900 locations and three prison sentences. This collaborative sting effort from the FBI and other countries shut down the website in 2015.

AlphaBay, launched in 2014, is another Dark Web Marketplace for illegal drugs and underground goods. In 2015, AlphaBay made news for selling stolen Uber accounts. Uber later said that they found no evidence of breach and alerted all the Uber users to use strong and unique usernames and passwords. In 2016, AlphaBay's API was compromised, leading to 13,000 messages being stolen. In 2017, The API was compromised, allowing over 200,000 private messages and a list of user names to be leaked. By July 2017, AlphaBay was ten times the size of the Silk Road.

According to the FBI, in early July 2017, multiple computer servers used by the AlphaBay website were seized worldwide, site creator and administrator, a 25 yr old Canadian living in Thailand, was arrested. Dark Web Wall Street Market was one of the markets on the darknet that specialized in digital goods and was created on a secure network with a quick and attractive trading products and payments system. It included a Unique award system, user rating system, and Exchangeable Image File Format (EXIF) remover for uploading images.

Wall Street Market was supposedly the second largest dark web marketplace in 2019. On May 3, 2019, there was a seizure notice from the police, saying that the platform and illegal content has been seized. German authorities seized the website and arrested its alleged operators in the process of exit-scamming when they were busted. The accused were not content to simply take a commission off the sale of drugs and stolen data but had decided to steal all their customers' cryptocurrency held in escrow. According to a study, Deep Web is 400-550 times bigger than the public internet; when someone searches on the internet, they access 0.03% or one in 3000 of the pages available.

Darknet or Dark Web is a subset of Deep Web; it's the most internal layer of the Onion. According to Wired, only about 0.01% of the deep web is the dark web. Google doesn't use index for shady websites, so you can't find any by using search engines. Once you are on the Dark Web, all illegal content is easily accessible. Before browsing, be aware of all the illicit activities and illicit businesses on the Dark Web. Journalists and whistleblowers also use the Dark Web to publish their thoughts which they can't do otherwise in their country. It isn't inherently illegal to go on the dark web if the intentions are good. It is used to keep internet activity anonymous and private, which can be helpful in both legal and illegal applications.

DeepFakes Deepfake is a 21st-century new name for the old traditional name Photoshopping. Deepfake uses a form of artificial intelligence called deep learning to make images of fake events. The idea of a person could be replaced with someone else's opinion; it's faking an image or the content. Deepfakes leverages powerful techniques from Artificial Intelligence (AI) and Machine Learning (ML). Fictional visuals, audio, and video content can be manipulated using machine learning methods based on deep learning, which involves training generative neural network architectures, such as generative adversarial networks(GAN) or autoencoders. The AI firm Deetrace found 15,000 deepfake videos online in September 2019, of which 99% of those mapped faces from female celebrities onto porn stars. Deepfake technology has been weaponized against women. Audi can be deep faked, too, by using "voice skins" or "voice clone." I

In 2018, US researchers discovered that deepfake faces don't blink normally, but as soon as they revealed this, it was fixed, and deepfakes appeared with flashing eyes. Politicians and celebrities are the most common victims of deepfakes; Peele's mouth was pasted on Obama's, which replaced Obama's jawline with Peele's mouth movements, then a fakeApp was used to refine the footage. Nancy Pelosi, the US House of the representative video, was slowed down by 25%, and the pitch was altered to make it look like she was slurring words.

High-profile figures are used because of the availability of their public profiles on the internet, which makes it easier for AI to learn from the ample source material available and accessible online. An average person takes so many selfies and posts them on social media public online; soon, anyone could be a victim of deepfakes. Deepfakes are finally forcing lawmakers to pay attention after years of activists fighting to protect victims of fake image-based violence. Parallel movements in the US and UK are gaining momentum to ban non-consensual deepfake images of women.

This attention could also ban other forms of image-based violence, which have been previously neglected. Microsoft has announced two-piece technology which aims to give necessary tools to users, which helps users filter out what's real and what's not. Microsoft video authenticator analyses images and videos to give a percentage chance or confidence score, that the media is artificially manipulated as per a blog on Microsoft's website. At the same time, the government and responsible companies are scrambling to find a solution to the deepfake problem. We need to be vigilant and watch out for our safety and reputation. In common law jurisdiction, the victim of deepfake can sue the deepfakes creator or publisher under one of the privacy torts, the most applicable of which is the "false light" theory. In US law,

The false light theory is a tort concerning privacy and defamation. It includes a non-public person's right to protection from publicity which puts the person in a false light. Under this theory, a plaintiff has to prove that the deepfake incorrectly represents the plaintiff in a way that would be embarrassing or offensive to the average person and could also amount to a defamation suit.

Chapter 10
Cyber Privacy

"Everyone is being watched; own Your Privacy."

Human dignity is inviolable. It must not be dishonored. Human dignity needs to be respected and protected. Human dignity involves personality rights, social media, and data collection about a person or internet user should be viewed in the context of human dignity. Innovative technology can infringe human dignity. Human dignity and privacy are inextricably linked to each other.

Every country and its laws give every citizen the right to their laws, human dignity, right to privacy, and right to develop their personality. With growing technology and an abundance of data breaches in recent years, privacy on the web has been discussed widely worldwide.

The world is waking up to the dangers of how modern technology can erode our privacy. We all leave digital traces while surfing the internet, some consciously and a lot more unconsciously. There are five popular U.S. tech companies Facebook, Apple, Amazon, Netflix, and Google (FAANG). FAANG acronym collectively indicates U.S. technology stocks of five major tech companies. GAFAM is also known acronym for five popular U.S. tech stocks - Google, Apple, Facebook, Amazon, and Microsoft (GAFAM).

Most net users tend to leave a lot of personal information and data while browsing these giant tech companies' websites. Facebook is known to collect more than 70% of the data; the Facebook-owned app contains more than 58% of all available data, including hobbies, height, weight, etc. Some of the other data-grabbing companies are Instagram, Tinder, Uber, Spotify, etc. Thanks to Facebook and Cambridge Analytica scandal saga for creating awareness. As per the studies conducted recently, we see that people trust less in social media with their sensitive data.

Cambridge Analytica, a data collector firm, gained access to information on 50 million Facebook users to identify the personalities of American voters and influence their behavior. President Trump hired a political data firm, Cambridge Analytica, in 2016 for an election campaign. This firm gained access to more than 50 million Facebook users and their personal information, helping the client to personalize the election campaign.

The data included users' identities, friends' networks, their "likes," etc. The idea was to map personality traits based on their internet usage behavior and then target audiences with personalized digital ads. These data collectors could add something to the data collected from users like the user's consumer numbers, their "likes," their "dislikes," and their internet usage behavior and resell it to anyone who wants to buy it for a price. We leave these enriched traces on the internet network, and algorithms use social sites to show relevant advertisements and videos to targeted customers.

In 2018, the harvesting of Facebook user's personal information by third-party apps at the center of the Cambridge Analytica privacy scandal was exposed. The response to this state of affairs has increased the number of new laws and regulations worldwide. A breakthrough privacy issue has come in General Data Protection Regulation (GDPR), considering it to be a new golden standard among data privacy regulations.

It is a European Union (E.U.) law that came into effect on May 25, 2018, which governs how personal data can be used, processed, and stored. It applies to all organizations within the E.U., as well as those supplying goods or services to the E.U. GDPR has seven fundamental principles, which are made part of U.K. law within the Data Protection Act (DPA) 2018:

- Lawfulness, transparency, and fairness.

- Propose limitation

- Data minimization

- Accuracy

- Storage limitation

- Integrity and confidentiality (security)

- Accountability. The GDPR applies to all 27 member countries of the European Union (E.U.).

The physical location is not necessary when considering whether GDPR covers it, but the area of the people whose data it handles is essential. Any company associated with E.U. companies to sell products or services should follow GDPR guidelines and be fully aware of GDPR. Many organizations that are likely to dismiss GDPR as irrelevant are not spared for the violation. The fines for non-compliance are hefty, either a fine of € 20 million or 4% of the company's annual turnover, whichever is higher. No matter which country an organization's headquarters, Ignorance about GDPR is not an acceptable excuse for violation; they are liable to be fined by the E.U. as long as they are associated or working with the E.U. companies.

Some countries already have existing agreements with the E.U. regarding the handling of data of E.U. citizens. The transfer of personal data outside the E.U. should adhere to an equivalent or high level of protection. To accommodate cross-border transfer outside the E.U., the European Commission provides adequacy decisions for specific countries. An adequacy decision permits cross-border, onward, and backward data transfer outside the E.U., without further authorization from a national supervisory authority (Article45(1), GDPR). It consists of an implementing act and an examination procedure, including criteria such as respect to the rule of law, access to justice, and international human rights. Privacy Shield is designed by the European Commission to protect the transfer of personal data to the U.S. The European Commission formally approved the EU-U.S. Privacy Shield framework in 2016 as an improved successor to the Safe harbor framework.

The International Safe Harbor Privacy principles were principles developed in the late 1990s, and early 2000's to prevent private organizations within the European Union or the United States which store customer data from accidentally disclosing or losing personal information. The Privacy Shield provided a voluntary certification program for which companies could sign up.

Companies applying for the certification program had to be qualified and commit themselves to Privacy Shield principles. Though the Court of Justice of the European Union (CJEU), on July 16, 2020, declared that the set of legal instruments called EU-US Privacy Shield invalid. Privacy Shield with standard contractual clauses is still valid for ensuring that a vendor provides the necessary data protection. Online data collection by digital companies and their capabilities to protect it is still under evaluation and is still not regulated at the federal level in the U.S. But different states are slowly embracing their policies to ensure that digital companies protect their users or provide more transparency.

In 2008, Illinois led the way with the Biometric Information Privacy Act. This law lets Illinois residents sue companies that collect their biometric data like face scans, fingerprints, palm prints, hand geography, etc., without their consent. After GDPR was passed in Europe in 2016 regulating their citizens' data protection, California decided to use it as a framework for its law.

The California Consumer Privacy Act (CCPA) took effect on January 01, 2020, protecting 40 million Americans living in California. CCPA gives consumers in that state rights regarding their data, and businesses face various obligations to comply. California consumers have a right to know what personal data is collected, used, shared, or sold by companies. They have the right to delete their data and the right to prohibit the sale of personal data. Businesses in California have many obligations, and they have to notify consumers in advance of the personal data being collected, they need to respond to consumers within specific time frames to the requests made by consumers under the act, they also have to disclose financial incentives offered in exchange for the retention or sale of personal data.

They have to keep the records of all requests made by consumers under the act and how they responded. They have to maintain data inventories, map data flows, and disclose data privacy policies and practices. California's law catalyzes the rest of the United States to be thinking deeply about data privacy. Nevada adopted the Privacy of Information collected on the internet from the consumers act in 2019, which allows the consumers in Nevada to opt out of personal data collection. Vermont passed a law in 2020 that requires data brokers to inform their consumers when personal information has been leaked or breached. In August 2020, Maine's new privacy law aimed squarely at Internet service providers, preventing them from sharing or selling consumers' data without explicit consent from the consumers. Virginia, Consumer Data Protection

The act was passed on March 02, 2021, making it the second state to enact comprehensive privacy legislation and the first one to do so on its initiative. Virginians will have the ability to access, correct, delete, and obtain a copy of personal data and opt-out of the processing of personal data for targeted advertising purposes, giving them many of the same data protection rights as California's Act. The New York Privacy Act, if enacted, would severely restrict how businesses can collect, use and share consumer data throughout the state. New York appears to be poised to make 2021 the year of data privacy for the Empire state by providing New Yorkers with transparency and control over their data and providing new privacy protections.

The New York Privacy Act replicates much of the E.U.'s GDPR. Still, it adds a private right of action, allowing individuals to bring lawsuits based on violations rather than relying on a governing body to do it. Assembly Bill 27, another law would amend New York's general business law to include a new biometric privacy act that guards against the nonconsensual-consensual of consumers' biometric identifiers. This law also empowers individuals to seek legal action for their rights being violated. Washington Data Privacy Act allows consumers to find out what data has been collected about them, ask for a copy of it, correct or delete that data, and have the data transferred to another platform. This bill was backed by the tech industry, created in collaboration with Amazon and Microsoft, so the critics called the bill "toothless" and preferred another bill to be passed. Another bill is called the People's Privacy Act, which is more explicit about biometric data rights and requires companies to obtain explicit consent before processing or sharing personal data.

Critics were again not clear how this will play out, So the state has taken the best practice of GDPR and the best practices of California law (CCPA) and the uniqueness of Washington and come up with an evidence-based best practices of a bill. The new rules would apply to companies that either does business in Washington or target state residents. Government agencies, processors of protected healthcare, and air carriers are exempt from the regulations. Utah passed the Electronic Information or Data Privacy Act in 2019, which required law enforcement to obtain a warrant before requesting personal data from companies. New Consumer Privacy Act, introduced on February 16, 2021, requires companies to provide transparency around private data collection and allows consumers to access, copy, and delete any personal data that a company collects about them. The law also empowers the attorney general to investigate a company's data practices. On March 04, 2021, The Oklahoma House of Representatives passed an opt-in data privacy bill called The Oklahoma Computer Data Privacy act, which requires internet technology companies to obtain explicit permission to collect and sell personal data.

The account is a heavily modified version of California's law (CCPA) for three reasons: Scope of applicability, consent for the collection, and opt-in to sales. There are several other bills currently on the docket in Alabama, Arizona, Florida, Connecticut, and Kentucky, all of which follow a similar format to California's CCPA. Strict data privacy legislation appears in more and more innovative economies globally—countries with GDPR-like Data Privacy Laws. Data Security executives globally adopt a cross-regulatory compliance strategy by determining how data privacy regulations overlap to synergize compliance efforts. Twelve countries have adopted or close to adopting data privacy laws similar to GDPR: Brazil, Australia, USA, Japan, South Korea, Thailand, Chile, New Zealand, India, South Africa, China, and Canada. All these countries have adopted similar privacy laws with slight variations.

All data privacy laws have two things in common: data protection and breach notification requirements; data-centric security can help every country and organization fulfill both requirements and develop a cross-regulatory compliance strategy that encompasses General Data Protection Regulation (GDPR) from E.U., California Consumer Privacy Act (CCPA) from California, Consumer Privacy Protection Act (CPPA) from Canada, Lei Geral de Protecao de Dados (LGPD) from Brazil, Personal Data Protection Law (PDPL) from China, Protection of Personal Information Act (POPIA) from South Africa and beyond.

References

Section – I

Chapter 1 - Evolution of Technology

https://www.msspalert.com/cybersecurity-breaches-and-attacks/5-most-common-web-application-attacks/

https://www.pentasecurity.com/blog/top-7-common-types-cyberattacks-web-applications/

Chapter 2 - Malware attack

https://tweaklibrary.com/cyber-threat-latest-computer-virus/

https://en.wikipedia.org/wiki/Rainbow_table

Chapter 3 - Introduction to Hacking and Ethical Hacking

https://hartmanadvisors.com/the-6-phases-of-an-incident-response-plan/

https://www.softwaretestinghelp.com/incident-response-service-providers/

https://www.softwaretestinghelp.com/incident-response-service-providers/

https://iot-analytics.com/state-of-the-iot-update-q1-q2-2018-number-of-iot-devices-now-7b/

https://dataprot.net/statistics/iot-statistics/

https://www.mckinsey.com/industries/semiconductors/our-insights/whats-new-with-the-internet-of-things

https://iotbusinessnews.com/2020/11/20/03121-global-iot-device-connections-to-reach-11-7-billion-in-2020-surpassing-non-iot-devices-for-the-first-time/

https://www.intellectsoft.net/blog/biggest-iot-security-issues/

https://campus.barracuda.com/product/webapplicationfirewall/doc/42049342/directory-traversal-vulnerability/

https://www.welivesecurity.com/2020/08/03/how-much-is-your-personal-data-worth-dark-web/

https://phoenixnap.com/blog/ransomware-examples-types

https://www.thesslstore.com/blog/difference-encryption-hashing-salting/

https://tools.cisco.com/security/center/resources/virus_differences

https://phoenixnap.com/blog/cyber-security-attack-types

https://www.isaca.org/resources/news-and-trend

https://industry-news/2020/top-cyberattacks-of-2020-and-how-to-build-cyberresiliency

https://devqa.io/types-of-hackers/

https://www.varonis.com/blog/cybersecurity-statistics/

Chapter 4 - Computer System Fundamentals

https://en.wikipedia.org/wiki/Operating_system

https://hostingtribunal.com/blog/operating-systems-market-share/#gref

https://www.solarwindsmsp.com/blog/types-of-network-security

https://whatismyipaddress.com/mac-address

https://www.binarytranslator.com/why-binary-numbers-are-used-by-computers#:~:text=Computers%20use%20voltages%20and%20since,use%20the%20binary%20number%20system.

Chapter 5 - Sniffers and Sniffing

https://www.softwaretestinghelp.com/network-packet-sniffers/#:~:text=SolarWinds%20Network%20Packet%20Sniffer%2C%20Wireshark,Kismet%20are%20completely%20free%20tools.&text=Many%20free%20and%20commercial%20packet%20analyzers%20are%20available%20in%20the%20market.

Chapter 6 - Social Engineering

https://www.securitymagazine.com/articles/94343-five-cyber-threats-to-watch-in-2021

https://portswigger.net/daily-swig/social-engineering

https://www.mcafee.com/blogs/other-blogs/mcafee-labs/2021-threat-predictions-report/

https://www.msspalert.com/cybersecurity-breaches-and-attacks/5-most-common-web-application-attacks/

https://www.pentasecurity.com/blog/top-7-common-types-cyberattacks-web-applications

Section - II

Chapter 7- Cyber Attack & Survival

https://www.kaspersky.com/about/press-releases/2021_share-of-account-takeover-incidents-increased-by-20-percentage-points

https://www.experian.com/blogs/ask-experian/20-types-of-identity-theft-and-fraud/

https://www.javelinstrategy.com/

https://www.cardrates.com/advice/credit-card-fraud-statistics/

Chapter 8 - Future Crimes

https://www.varonis.com/blog/cybersecurity-statistics/

https://www.splunk.com/en_us/form/top-50-security-threats.html?utm_campaign=google_amer_en_search_generic_security&utm_source=google&utm_medium=cpc&utm_content=top_50_sec_thrts_EB&utm_term=cyberthreat&_bk=cyberthreat&_bt=476981134771&_bm=p&_bn=g&_bg=102227774800&device=c&gclid=CjwKCAjw3pWDBhB3EiwAV1c5rFyr8Msu0mgkA-A9EWncWvVNmJ6iLddh-mLauqbNIb2JPK4ZjB7gsRoC_m4QAvD_BwE

https://www.forbes.com/sites/johnkoetsier/2020/09/26/global-online-content-consumption-doubled-in-2020/?sh=7972ac72fdeb

https://www.splunk.com/pdfs/ebooks/top-50-security-threats.pdf

https://www.security.org/digital-safety/

https://www.salesforce.com/products/platform/best-practices/benefits-of-cloud-computing/

https://www.cloudflare.com/learning/cloud/what-is-the-cloud/

https://safeatlast.co/blog/ransomware-statistics/#gref

https://safeatlast.co/

https://learn-umbrella.cisco.com/ebook-library/ransomware-defense-for-dummies-2nd-edition

https://boozallen.com/content/dam/boozallen_site/ccg/pdf/publications/cyber-threat-trends-outlook-2021.pdf

https://monstercloud.com/surveys/monstercloud-reviews-top-ransomware-threats-for-2021/

https://www.boozallen.com/c/insight/publication/8-cyber-threat-trends-for-2021.html

https://www.boozallen.com/c/insight/publication/8-cyber-threat-trends-for-2021.html#:~:text=The%20report%20covers%208%20key,via%20Cloud%2DHosted%20Development%20Environments&text=Mandated%20Contact%20Tracing%20Apps%20May%20Open%20Doors%20for%20Large%2DScale%20Cyber%20Attacks

Chapter 9 - Deep Web and Deepfake

https://iapp.org/news/a/privacy-law-and-resolving-deepfakes-online/

https://en.wikipedia.org/wiki/Deepfake

https://mashable.com/article/dark-web-market-wallstreet-seized-police/

https://www.fbi.gov/news/stories/alphabay-takedown

https://quod.lib.umich.edu/j/jep/3336451.0007.104?view=text;rgn=main#:~:text=The%20deep%20Web%20contains%207%2C500,deep%20Web%20sites%20presently%20exist.

https://en.wikipedia.org/wiki/Playpen_(website)

https://www.soscanhelp.com/what-is-the-dark-web-definitive-guide

https://en.wikipedia.org/wiki/Silk_Road_(marketplace)

Chapter 10 - Cyber Privacy

https://insights.comforte.com/12-countries-with-gdpr-like-data-privacy-laws

https://www.defensorum.com/gdpr-countries-list/

https://www.fastcompany.com/90606571/state-data-privacy-laws-2021

https://le.utah.gov/~2021/bills/static/SB0200.html

https://www.jdsupra.com/legalnews/oklahoma-house-passes-computer-data-5745855/

https://americaninnovators.com/news/2021-data-privacy/

https://www.ghostery.com/4-free-ways-to-own-your-privacy-on-data-privacy-day-2021/

https://insights.comforte.com/canadas-new-data-privacy-bill-the-digital-charter-information-act

https://www.coursera.org/learn/history-privacy-laws/supplement/FxMvq/addicted-to-fake-news-violation-of-human-dignity

https://www.businessofapps.com/data/facebook-statistics/

https://bgr.com/2021/01/05/app-privacy-labels-facebook-messenger-vs-imessge-signal-whatsapp/

https://cloud.google.com/solutions/education

Glossary

Abnormal: Deviating from what is normal or usual, typically in a way that is undesirable or worrying

Abstraction: The quality of dealing with ideas rather than events. Accelerate: Increase in rate, amount, or extent.

Adequate: Satisfactory or acceptable in quality or quantity.

Aggressors: Feelings of anger or antipathy resulting in hostile or violent behavior; readiness to attack or confront.

AI *Artificial intelligence* (*AI*): Intelligence demonstrated by machines, unlike the natural intelligence displayed by humans and animals

Authentication: The process or action of verifying the identity of a user or process.

Bandwidth: A range of frequencies within a given band is used for transmitting a signal.

Biometrics: Physical or behavioral human characteristics that can be used to digitally identify a person to grant access to systems, devices, or data

Breach: Infraction or violation of a law, obligation, tie

Brute-force relying on or achieved through the application of **force**

Cache: A thing that is hidden or stored somewhere, or to the place where it is hidden

Catalyst: A substance that enables a chemical reaction to proceed at a usually faster rate or under different conditions (as at a lower temperature) than otherwise possible.

Coax: Obtain something from (someone) by gentle and persistent persuasion. Coerce: Persuade (an unwilling person) to do something by using force or threats.

Collision: An instance of two or more records being assigned the same identifier or location in memory.

Congestion: A network state where a node or link carries so much data that it may deteriorate network service quality, resulting in queuing delay, frame or data packet loss, and the blocking of new connections.

Conspicuous: Not clearly visible.

Cryptographic: The art of writing or solving codes.

Database: A structured set of data held in a computer, especially one that is accessible in various ways

Delineate: Describe, portray, or set forth with accuracy or in detail Demodulate: Extract or separate (a modulating signal) from its carrier

Digitization: The process of converting information into a digital (i.e., computer-readable) format.

Disposal: The action or process of getting rid of something.

Disruption: Disturbance or problems which interrupt an event, activity, or process. Eavesdropping: Secretly listening to a conversation.

Encryption: The method by which information is converted into secret code hides the information's true meaning.

Escalation: A rapid increase; a rise.

Exabyte: A unit of measurement for computers of the future. One **exabyte** holds 1000 petabytes (PB) or a million trillion (1,000,000,000,000,000,000) bytes.

Explicit: Fully and clearly expressed or demonstrated Exploit: Make full use of and derive benefit from (a resource)

Extortion: The practice of obtaining something, especially money, through force or threats

Extraction: Not allowed or permitted, usually because it's seen to be irrelevant Fraudster: A person who commits fraud, especially in business dealings.

Fraudulent: Obtained, done by, or involving deception, especially criminal Deception: Frazzled showing the effects of exhaustion or strain

Genetic engineering: **Genetic engineering** uses recombinant DNA (rDNA) technology to alter the **genetic** makeup of an organism.

Geofencing: the use of GPS or RFID technology to create a virtual geographic boundary, enabling software to trigger a response when a mobile device enters or leaves a particular area.

Gibberish: Speech that is (or appears to be) nonsense. A high level of granularity characterizes granularity.

Hijack: Take over (something) and use it for a different purpose. Impersonation: Pretends to be (another person) for entertainment or fraud.

Inextricably: In a way that is impossible to disentangle or separate. Infectious: Likely to spread or influence others in a rapid manner.

Initiation: The action of beginning something.

Integral: Necessary to make a whole complete; essential or fundamental.

Interception: The action or fact of preventing someone or something from continuing to a destination.

IoT, **Internet of Things (IoT)**: It refers to a system of interrelated, internet-connected objects that can collect and transfer data over a wireless network without human intervention.

Jeopardy: Exposure to or imminence of death, loss, or injury

Keylogger: A computer program that records every keystroke made by a computer user, especially to gain fraudulent access to passwords and other confidential information.

Legislation: Law that has been promulgated (or "enacted") by a **legislature** or other governing body or the process of making it

Legitimate: Conforming to the law or rules.

Lure: Tempt (a person or animal) to do something or to go somewhere, especially by offering some form of reward.

Lurking: Remaining hidden to wait in ambush

Malicious having or showing a desire to cause harm to someone

Malware: The collective name for several malicious software variants, including viruses, ransomware, and spyware.

Memory: The ability to stay in the computer's **memory** after execution and to continuously run.

Methodology: A system of methods used in a particular area of study or activity.

Misconfiguration: An incorrect or inappropriate configuration.

Mitigation: Makes (something bad) less severe, serious, or painful. Nonconsensual: Not agreed to by one or more of the people involved.

Nullify: Make legally null and void; invalidate

Obstruction. A thing that impedes or prevents passage or progress; an obstacle or blockage.

OSI Open Systems Interconnection (**OSI**): A model describes seven layers that computer systems use to communicate over a network

Penetrate: Gain access to (an organization, place, or system), especially when this is difficult to do.

Persuade: To move by argument, request, or expostulation to a belief, position, or course of action.

Phishing: The fraudulent practice of sending emails purporting from reputable companies to induce individuals to reveal personal information, such as passwords and credit card numbers.

Probe: A thorough investigation into a crime or other matter.

Propagate: Spread and promote (an idea, theory, etc.) widely.

Provocations: Speech that makes someone angry, especially deliberately.

Quantum: Quantum **is the** Latin **word** for amount and, in modern understanding, **means** the smallest possible discrete unit of any physical property, such as energy or matter.

Rampant: Flourishing or spreading unchecked.

Ransomware: A type of malicious software designed to block access to a computer system until a sum of money is paid.

Remediation: The act of remedying or correcting something that has been corrupted or that is deficient

Repetitive: Containing or characterized by repetition, especially when unnecessary or tiresome. Repudiation: Rejection of a proposal or idea.

Resilient (of a substance or object): Able to recoil or spring back into shape after bending, stretching, or compressing.

Retransmits: rebroadcast or send out (an electrical signal or a radio or television program).

Retrieve: The action of obtaining or consulting material stored in a computer system.

Robust: Strong and healthy; vigorous

Segment each of the parts into which something is or may be divided.

Self-replicate any behavior of a dynamical system that yields construction of an identical or similar copy of itself.

Sniffing: A process of monitoring and capturing all data packets passing through a given network.

Snooping: The action of furtively trying to find out something, especially information about someone's private affairs.

Spammers: A person or organization that sends irrelevant or unsolicited messages over the internet.

Spoof: A specific type of cyber-attack in which someone attempts to use a **computer**, device, or network to trick other **computer** networks by masquerading as a legitimate entity.

Standalone (of computer hardware or software): able to operate independently of other hardware or software.

Subnetting: The technique for logically partitioning a single physical network into multiple smaller sub-networks or **subnets**

Suicide hackers: A **hacker** who hacks for the sake of destruction.

Surveillance: Close observation, especially of a suspected spy or criminal.

Tampering: Interference with (something) to cause damage or make unauthorized alterations.

Tedious: Too long, slow, or dull; tiresome or monotonous.

UEBA: **User and Entity Behavior Analytics** and was previously known as **user behavior analytics** (UBA).

Vector: An organism, typically a biting insect or tick, transmits a disease or parasite from one animal or plant to another.

Vigilant: Keeping careful watch for possible danger or difficulties.

VPN "**Virtual Private Network**" describes the opportunity to establish a protected network connection when using public networks.

www.ingramcontent.com/pod-product-compliance
Lightning Source LLC
LaVergne TN
LVHW060123070326
832902LV00019B/3104